Pregnant and Single

Help for the Tough Choices

Revised Edition

Linda Roggow & Carolyn Owens

Herald
Press

Scottdale, Pennsylvania
Waterloo, Ontario

Library of Congress Cataloging-in-Publication Data
Roggow, Linda.
Pregnant and single : help for tough choices / Linda Roggow and Carolyn Owens. — Rev. ed.
p. cm.
Includes bibliographical references.
ISBN 0-8361-9092-0 (alk. paper)
1. Unmarried mothers—United States. 2. Pregnancy, Unwanted—United States. 3. Teenage mothers—United States. 4. Teenage pregnancy—United States. I. Owens, Carolyn Pearl. II. Title.
HQ759.45.R64 1998
362.83'92'08352—dc21 98-21074

Paper in this publication is recycled and meets the minimum requirements of American National Standard for Information Sciences—Permanence of Paper for Printed Library Materials, ANSI Z39.48-1984.

Scripture credits appear on page 6.
Earlier editions of this book by Zondervan Publishing House:
Handbook for Pregnant Teenagers, 1984.
Pregnant and Single, 1990.

PREGNANT AND SINGLE

Library of Congress Catalog Number: 98-21074
International Standard Book Number: 0-8361-9092-0
Printed in the United States of America
Book and cover design by Paula M. Johnson

07 06 05 04 03 02 01 00 99 98 10 9 8 7 6 5 4 3 2 1

To—

Our parents,
Bette and Bud Florine,
Pearl and Roland Starry.
Thank you for giving us life.

Our husbands,
Paul Roggow,
Bill Owens.
Thank you to the two men who
lovingly cheered us on.

Our grandmothers
Esther Florine,
Bernice Pool.
Thank you for the wonderful
influence you've had on our lives.

Scripture Credits

Contents

Preface

THROUGHOUT OUR LIVES, we move through phases, some good, some difficult. For many of the young women with whom I have worked, a pregnancy outside of marriage seemed more than they could bear. I witnessed how they moved through this difficult phase to gain more maturity, understanding of themselves, and a deeper appreciation for how God can work in their lives.

In Jeremiah 29:11-14 the Lord declares, "I know the plans I have for you, . . . plans for your welfare and not for harm, to give you a future with hope. Then when you call upon me and come and pray to me, I will hear you. When you search for me, you will find me; if you seek me with all your heart, I will let you find me."

God has a plan for each of us, even during the trying phases of our lives. He can turn a bad situation into a good one.

I have deep respect for each woman who makes the decision to carry her baby to term, even though her circumstances are less than desirable. I appreciate the many women who have shared their stories to teach and encourage others.

All names have been changed to keep things confidential. I hope our book will help to guide you through your decision-making process and toward a better understanding of God's perfect plan for you.

—Linda Riggow, MSW, LISW
Jackson, Minnesota

• • •

There are times when we don't know where to turn. Life seems overwhelming, decision making almost impossible.

We pray that this book, with its straightforward discussion, will point you toward your best decision.

—Carolyn Owens
Minneapolis, Minnesota

1

Don't Panic!

JILL, TWENTY-ONE YEARS OLD, has just completed her junior year at a state university. Since her sophomore year in high school, Jill has been active in church groups. Now she is a leader of a Christian group on her campus. But today none of those things is important.

Jill is pregnant—and unmarried.

This morning she is determined to keep an appointment, her third, at the abortion clinic. She canceled the other two. Why? She wasn't sure she wanted an abortion. But this appointment she intends to keep.

She sits on the edge of her bed in the dorm room, struggling to wipe away the tears that run down her face. Jill's thoughts echo voices from the past that gossiped about another young woman in similar straits:

"Did you hear about ________________?"

"No! Really! That's terrible! I never would have believed it."

As she caresses the cameo rose pendant Randy gave her less than three months ago, Jill catches a glimpse of a large poster on her dorm wall. It's of her and Randy looking happy, carefree, and much in love.

Why me? Why did this happen to me?

Her thoughts begin to race: *People at home will say, "How could a nice young woman like Jill get into a mess like this?" Just wait till my friends find out. They'll never understand. I'll lose their respect.*

Then she tries to reason things out: *I'm too young to be a parent. I want to have fun. Share good times with my friends. Go out on dates.*

Feelings of panic grip her again. Thinking about all the rumors that will spread, Jill hates the box she has put herself in. *If only I hadn't let Randy sweet-talk me, this wouldn't have happened. "Love!"* She spits the word out. It tastes bitter and slimy.

Jill knows she can't go through with this pregnancy. She'd have to leave college. How would she support herself? What about all the medical expenses? She must go through with this abortion.

After all, she reminds herself, *it's just a problem for today. Tomorrow the baby will be gone. Baby?* Suddenly she remembers why she canceled the last two appointments. *Abortion means taking a human life. I can't go through with that. I just can't.*

But how can I tell my parents? They'll be hurt . . . horrified . . . ashamed. Who knows what they'll think or how they'll react? How can I give them this grief? How can I even face them?

She struggles some more. *But if I go through with the abortion, how can I face God or myself?* Jill looks at the phone. . . .

The Cycle of Sorrow

If you're in the same situation as Jill, in the next few days, weeks, and months, your emotions and physical condition will go through some changes. Let's face it: you're never going to be the same person you were before pregnancy. You may experience quickly shifting moods. At this moment, your hormones are adjusting to body changes.

Lots of women tend to be more emotional right before their periods, with ups and downs. You may experience those same kinds of intense feelings now. One day you may feel anxious and unsure. The next, you may be exuberant and feel more womanly, more feminine.

At times, depending on your emotions and attitude, you may believe you're embarking on a new adventure. Other times, if your mood is down, you're sure you should never have been born. You'll think any other crisis is less difficult than the situation you are in now!

In any crisis there is a seven-step Cycle of Sorrow. The seven steps are (1) shock, (2) denial, (3) anger, (4) bargaining, (5) depression, (6) acceptance, and (7) growth. Some of these steps can overlap. We will observe this cycle through the eyes of a pregnant young woman.

1. Shock

Holly felt immobilized. She heard the doctor say, "You're pregnant," but she couldn't believe it. She didn't "feel" pregnant.

Shock serves as a cushion, giving Holly time to absorb the fact of pregnancy. "I remember how I felt when the doctor told me," she said. "I was speechless! The shock waves were almost visible. I went home and couldn't talk or eat. All I could manage to do was stare off into space."

Shock is a defense mechanism, a buffer against the crisis. However, shock leaves as rapidly as one is able to absorb the painful reality.

2. Denial

Denial can last for twenty-four hours or as long as the entire pregnancy. Holly wanted to deny the circumstances.

She didn't even want to think about a baby coming in nine months. Her mind fixed on one thought: *This is just a temporary inconvenience.*

"My denial mechanism was super strong," Holly remembered. "I was an aerobics instructor and wasn't about to give it up. But in my fourth month, I saw how my body was changing, and I could no longer deny reality."

Sometimes a woman thinks that no one will ever find out, that the pregnancy will not affect her lifestyle. But if she thinks she can get through the pregnancy without telling those closest to her, she is not being realistic. She needs emotional support especially at this time. Even though everything within her wants to deny the pregnancy, it's better to get the crisis out in the open.

3. Anger

Holly's denial turned into anger: "I can't believe I got caught! It just isn't fair. Most of my friends aren't virgins. In fact, I know a lot of them really sleep around a lot. Why me?"

She became angry with God, her parents, and her boyfriend, but mostly with herself.

"Talk about stupid! Why did I ever listen to Bill? Now I'm the one in trouble, and he goes on his merry way."

4. Bargaining

Then Holly tried to strike a bargain with God. "Please, let this be all a big mistake," she pleaded. "If you make it disappear, I'll keep sex for marriage from now on."

She prayed for the natural disaster of a miscarriage. Holly didn't realize that bargaining is really an attempt to postpone the inevitable.

5. Depression

Depression can come at any time during a pregnancy. You may have an overwhelming sense of hopelessness and despair, a strong feeling that there is no solution. Holly became confused. She had trouble getting up for work, and when she arrived at her job, she couldn't concentrate.

This feeling of futility can become so extreme that the person no longer thinks rationally. Some young women become so depressed that they attempt suicide.

6. Acceptance

"In the middle of my fourth month, I came to the conclusion that I had better get help," Holly said. "I'd worked through the denial, anger, bargaining, and depression. Then I realized it was time to face my pregnancy and accept it.

"No matter how hard I prayed, I knew it wasn't going to go away. There wasn't going to be any miscarriage."

At that point, Holly told a close friend. After many tears and a lot of honest dialogue, her friend encouraged her to seek counseling.

7. Growth

"I believe these last few months have been some of the hardest I'll ever have to go through," Holly admitted.

"But having worked through the previous six stages, I'm now heading toward a positive resolution. For the first time, with my counselor's help and my friend's support, I can see a glimmer of light at the end of the tunnel."

It's Okay to Have Feelings!

You may be hurting right now. You may feel like kicking someone or doing something worse. It may feel like the end of the world. Your future may seem bleak and hopeless. Give yourself permission to hurt and be angry. It's okay to feel that way. It is also important to learn how to cope with your stress in one of the most difficult times of your life.

Ways People Cope

In this time when you are feeling so sensitive and uncertain, you can be open to learning how to cope effectively. According to Gerald Caplan's crisis theory, the new pattern of coping that you work out to deal with this crisis can become a valuable way to solve future problems. There are healthy and unhealthy ways to cope.[1]

Unhealthy Ways to Cope

- Deny that a problem exists: *I'll wear loose, cover-up clothes.*
- Refuse to seek or accept help: *I'll handle it myself.*
- Run away from it: *I'll get high to escape and forget.*
- Fail to explore alternatives: *I've already made up my mind.*
- Blame others: *It's all his fault.*
- Turn away from friends and family: *Everyone just leave me alone!*

Healthy Ways to Cope

- Face the problem.
- Gain a better perspective on it.
- Work through bad feelings.

- Accept responsibility for coping with the problem.
- Explore different ways to handle the crisis.
- Figure out the difference between what can be changed and what cannot be changed.
- Be open to communicating with people who are ready to give support.
- Take steps, however small, to handle the crisis positively.

How Can You Cope?

Likely your first reaction to being pregnant was this: "Help! Someone get me out of this mess!" You may think that you are at a dead end, with no way out. However, this moment—the first explosion of your crisis—is the worst possible time to make any final decisions.

Today you are under much stress and pressure. Your coping abilities may be weak right now. Move slowly toward any solution. "Take one day at a time" is a bit of wisdom you will want to practice all the time.

Positive Actions to Help You Cope

Here are some things you can do to combat your negative emotions. Participating in one or all of these will help you calm your thoughts. They will also help you to see your situation more clearly.

- Practice relaxation exercises.
- Take warm baths.
- Sit back and take deep breaths.
- Go for long walks.
- Pray.

Jill takes a deep breath and calls the abortion clinic to cancel her appointment. Then she dials again, this time a number she had copied from a poster on her dormitory bulletin board.

A woman answers, "Pregnancy care center."

Pregnant and single, Jill is not alone. Lots of other single women are in crisis pregnancies, too. In the United States, more than a million single women become pregnant each year, and the number is increasing rapidly.

A Word About Abortion

For many, abortion looks like the easiest way out: no one would have to know, and life might go on as usual. Some live with this "secret" deep in the depths of their hearts. The reality of abortion may not surface until years later.

Before she makes this decision, a woman can have an ultrasound to see exactly what type of "tissue" will be removed. "Seeing one's unborn child in the uterus is an indescribable experience, as awesome as Earth seen from the moon, or Jupiter's Great Red Spot. Seen on the ultrasound screen, the fetus waves, kicks, and swivels in the amniotic sac."[2]

Truthfully, abortion is a surgical procedure. Anytime a person has surgery, it is wise to know exactly what's involved and to understand the associated risks. When the procedure is an abortion, you need to know that it destroys the life that lives within the woman's body. This fact can cause a woman emotional pain and suffering for years to come.

From a spiritual standpoint, abortion conflicts with God's will. *God is the Life-Giver*. We were created to respect life and reverence our Creator. "Reverence for the Lord is a fountain of life" (Proverbs 14:27, TLB).

2

What's Happening to Me?

You are probably aware that many physical changes occur throughout pregnancy. If you need more specific information, this chapter is for you.

Something's Missing

In many but not all cases, the first change you noticed was that your monthly flow stopped. If you had sexual intercourse, then missed a menstrual period after regular cycles, pregnancy is the most likely cause.

Filling Out

Another physical change will be enlarged breasts due to lactation. Liquid forming inside the breasts will increase their size throughout pregnancy. In the beginning they will be tender, but later the sensitivity and tingling sensation will disappear.

Your breasts may leak a fluid called colostrum. In the first few months, it will look yellow and watery. However, toward the end of term, the colostrum takes on an opaque, whitish appearance and resembles milk.

Upset Stomach

You may experience morning sickness. The nausea, sometimes with vomiting, can occur at any time of the day.

Although the cause is not known, some doctors think it is a result of hormonal changes occurring at the beginning of pregnancy. Usually morning sickness disappears at the end of the first trimester.

During this time, you may find that some foods or aromas you have always enjoyed will cause nausea. It is a good idea to eat soda crackers and divide your food into several small meals a day. One caution: A pregnant woman must *never* take any medicine without her doctor's permission.

Tired All the Time

Some women feel great fatigue. At first you may feel as though you cannot force yourself out of bed. You may be tired all day and want long afternoon naps. Generally this need for extra sleep disappears after the first few months.

Bathroom Visits

Many women need to urinate frequently. This is caused by the growing baby crowding the bladder. The condition usually goes away after the tenth or twelfth week. It often recurs a few weeks before delivery.

Round and Firm, but Not Flat

As your baby continues to grow, you will see your abdomen gradually enlarging. You will first notice this around the twelfth week. Sometime between week sixteen and week twenty, you will begin to "show," enough for others to notice.

Streaks may form on one side or both sides of your abdomen. These stretch marks will look pearl-white. They will turn pale after pregnancy, but they will never totally disappear.

All these changes are definite signs that you are pregnant. At this stage, you may not be thinking about whether your baby has brown or blue eyes; you may not wonder if his or her hair is red, black, or blond. More important things are happening.

With each day that passes, your child is being formed in fine detail. The baby's eyes, facial features, arms, and legs are developing in your womb. This is the way each of us was "fearfully and wonderfully made, . . . intricately woven" inside our mothers (Psalm 139:13-16).

To help in this development, you will want to do everything necessary to ensure that the two of you, baby and mother, come through this pregnancy in the best possible condition. In the next chapter, we will discuss ways to accomplish this.

3

Healthy Mother and Baby

SOCIETY IN GENERAL AND MEDICAL experts in particular are learning more about how an unborn child is affected by the mother's health care. As you begin to feel and see signs of pregnancy, it's important to seek good medical attention. We urgently advise you to *see a doctor*.

See a Doctor!

"Numerous studies show that mothers who have early, and regular prenatal care are more likely to have healthy babies than women who have little or no care. Premature or low-birth-weight babies occur two to three times more often for women who have had inadequate care."[1]

Teenage pregnancy is a high-risk situation. Nearly half of young pregnant women receive no prenatal care in their first three months. However, you will automatically lower the risk when you have regular checkups with a competent obstetrician. Such prenatal visits are covered by most health insurance plans (see chapter 8).

In prenatal care your doctor will inform you about times and locations of childbirth classes. Among other things, those classes can teach you relaxation exercises.

Your doctor will educate you in what to do and what not to do during pregnancy. After all, "The birth of a child, a new life, . . . is one of the most profound and important events that can happen. . . .

"A young woman can increase her chances of producing a healthy, normal baby by knowing exactly what things can threaten her baby's development and then by avoiding them. In this way, she is already protecting and nurturing her child; in this way, she is already a good mother."[2]

Here are some facts to help you and your baby stay healthy during pregnancy.

Nutrition During Pregnancy

You may never have thought much about nutrition before you were pregnant. Now it is doubly important to eat well-balanced meals.

Pregnancy is a time of such rapid growth and development that it demands good nutrition. The pregnant woman needs to take care of nutritional requirements for both herself and her baby.

Healthy eating can prevent or lessen many of the common problems faced by mother and child. Every woman, no matter what her weight before pregnancy, needs to gain enough weight to maintain her health and the baby's well-being during the pregnancy.

To ensure good health and nutrition for you and your child, eat a variety of foods. Go easy on snack foods and sweets or the pounds will appear faster than you'd like.

Of course, the proper amount of weight gain will vary with each person. Your doctor will tell you what your gain should be. Whether great or small, this is not the time to go on a crash diet.

Drugs During Pregnancy

This is extremely IMPORTANT: Do not take any drugs or medicines in any form unless your doctor tells you to take them. This rule applies to illegal drugs, prescription medicines, medicines you can buy at the drugstore without prescriptions, and vitamins and herbs. Your doctor is the expert in this area.

Caffeine

Did you know that caffeine is a drug and has been part of the human diet for several thousand years?

Caffeine is a natural ingredient in coffee, tea, chocolate, cocoa, and some soft drinks. When a pregnant woman drinks or eats caffeine, it goes from her body to her unborn child. Caffeine has also been detected in the milk of breast-feeding mothers.[3] Caffeine is not good for children, born or unborn.

Alcohol

Alcohol is also considered a drug. Lots of people use it as a form of escape. As a pregnant woman, you need the facts: "One to three out of every 1,000 newborns, or about 5,000 babies per year, are born with fetal alcohol syndrome (FAS). A new study points out that even two or three drinks a week may trigger spontaneous abortion.

"Since no one knows at which point in the pregnancy alcohol does the greatest damage or what amount can be consumed safely, pregnant women should drink no alcoholic beverages."[4]

Cigarettes

One warning on cigarette packages says that smoking may complicate pregnancy. Babies born to smokers usually weigh a half pound less than babies born to nonsmokers. Low-birth-weight babies are forty times more likely to die in infancy than those of normal weight.

The nicotine in cigarettes constricts blood vessels. That may reduce blood flow from mother to baby, thus reducing the amounts of nutrients and oxygen to the unborn baby. Smoking may also increase the risk of miscarriage, stillbirth, and death in newborns.[5]

There are many harmful things that can endanger your baby's health and your health. However, the question of whom you should tell can seem even more dangerous to you than the matter of what to eat.

4

Who Can I Turn To?

You Are Not Alone

Being pregnant and single affects women from all areas of society, all economic levels, and all nationalities. Every woman who is pregnant and single lives her own real-life drama of mental, physical, and emotional strain. Each one faces the same choices.

If you are pregnant, young, and unmarried, you may be living at home, be away at school, or perhaps be out on your own with a job. You are likely afraid, confused, and torn by many emotions.

Where do you go from here? To whom can you turn? Don't despair! Your future is changed, but not finished. With careful thought and some help, good opportunities are still ahead.

Who Should I Tell?

You are probably anxious to tell someone about your pregnancy, yet afraid. Soon you are going to have to tell someone. At this point, you need to think carefully about who you tell.

As soon as you tell, you'll be bombarded with opinions about your situation. People will want to tell you what to do. Therefore, you need to determine who should be told first and prepare yourself for their reaction.

Parents

The logical place to begin, of course, is with your parents, as difficult as that may be. For instance, you may think your parents will be violently angry, perhaps so angry that they will disown you.

You can expect that they will be hurt at first. Parents tend to blame themselves when things like this happen. They will probably say, "Where have we gone wrong? What did we do to deserve this?"

Your pregnancy is a crisis in their lives as well as in yours. Do you remember how you felt when you first found out? They will have many of those same feelings. They will go through their own Cycle of Sorrow (see chapter 1).

Some parents will try to take over the decision making completely. Some may say, "You're going to have an abortion, and that's final!" They may not actually mean that. That could be their first reaction because they're so used to protecting you.

No one can *force* you to have an abortion against your will. Remember that your parents are also in shock. Give them time and space to sort through their feelings.

Do you recall a time from your earlier years when you told your parents something with fear and trembling? Maybe your parents discovered something on their own—that you dented the car, lied, or cheated on a test?

Did your parents come through for you then? If so, there's a good possibility that, after their initial shock, they'll again come through with the support you need.

You could begin the conversation like this: "Mom, Dad, I love you, but I've really let you down. I'm sorry to have to tell you this. . . ."

On the other hand, maybe you will think it best to speak with one parent at a time or to tell an older brother or sister first. However, if you simply cannot bear the thought of dealing with the reactions of your family now, how about talking with . . .

A Trusted Friend?

Can you think of someone you feel comfortable confiding in? This might be someone with whom you've shared good times and bad, laughter and tears. You know the friend so well that you feel confident the person won't be shocked or criticize you. This is the friend to confide in.

Your Boyfriend?

What about the father of your baby? Will he stand with you or against you? In your mind, picture his reaction. Will he act unsure? Deny everything? Refuse to take any responsibility? Do you think he'll be pleased, proud, protective, and loving?

Whatever his reaction is, it's important for the two of you to be alone when you tell him. He also needs time to sort through his feelings. After you've talked, meet again later, after he's had a chance to think about it.

However, the father is not the person to make final decisions. That's for you to do, and if you are underage (of 18 years, generally), you will need to do this in consultation with your parents and/or the court. If the father of the baby insists that you abort, patiently explain that his opinion is important, but that you are the one carrying the child. If your boyfriend still lives at home, you may want to include his parents in this discussion after the two of you have discussed it alone.

When you meet with your boyfriend, get your feelings out in the open and find out what support you have. When you get together to discuss the problem, you both can gain a clearer perspective of how the two of you think and feel. In most cases, one set of parents will take a firm stand right away. They might control the situation if the two of you are not sure of your feelings.

You and your boyfriend will need to discuss who is going to pay the medical bills. What about the relationship? Will it be continued? These discussions will help provide direction for you and your boyfriend, as well as for your families. (Also see chapter 12.)

People in Your Church?

If you are involved in a church, one of the scariest things is wondering what the people there will say and think. How can you face them? If possible, talk with one of the spiritual leaders. Your pastor should be able to recommend a trained professional to counsel you if the church does not have a trained counselor. Your health insurance might provide some coverage for counseling.

If you don't have a church family, this is a good time to find one. Do you have good friends who attend church? You could visit their churches with them. You may feel like withdrawing from the human race, but seclusion won't help. You need caring and concerned people.

Dealing with Others' Reactions

As your pregnancy progresses and more people find out, you will probably meet many reactions, ranging from total acceptance to shock and heavy blaming. You will have to get used to the idea that some people won't accept your pregnancy. Other people's negative feelings about your situation may sometimes be the hardest thing you have to handle.

People's reactions come from their own backgrounds and values. Many of them will try to suggest what you should do, and you know they mean well. However, their suggestions may not fit you. After you have considered their advice, make your own decisions.

Some of your friends and peers may actually turn against you and reject you. They just can't deal with your pregnancy. They may be afraid it could happen to them. Your acceptance of their feelings may help them, in time, to accept your feelings.

Where Will I Live?

Some of you will choose to live at home, but for others, that will not be an option. Your parents might feel you can't stay there while you're pregnant, or you may not be comfortable living with them.

You may decide to stay with a relative. Perhaps you will need to find other living arrangements. Could you stay with a friend for a while?

If that's unlikely, the National Citizens Concerned for Life, centered in Washington, D.C., has developed a network of pregnancy care centers in the United States and Canada. The centers have "shepherding homes" available for unwed mothers. These homes are loving, concerned families, prepared to help women in a crisis pregnancy. The back of this book lists such resources.

What About School?

If you are still in school, you may wonder whether you have to quit. In most schools, you may continue as long as your doctor approves. If the doctor says you must stay at home, ask the school to provide tutoring for you. It might be an option for you to be tutored at home earlier, if that is what you want and if you can pay for it.

There are also schools just for pregnant young women. In some states they are called continuing education or family education centers, and they differ from regular high school. The curriculum includes practical, realistic options for pregnant students. These schools give instructon in—

- academic courses.
- prenatal and postnatal care.
- family relations.
- homemaking.
- money and time management.
- career development and personal guidance.

Such centers offer opportunity for peer interaction. The program may last about sixteen weeks, with classes held Monday through Friday, six hours a day. At many of the centers, expectant fathers and future grandparents may also be involved.

Some areas provide a mentoring program that matches teen mothers with successful women in business. The mentors regularly relate with the students and share encouragement, advice, and help.

If you are in college, you should be able to continue your schedule. You may wish to discuss this with your adviser. If you are working, find out if you are eligible for paid maternity leave, insurance, and health benefits.

In this chapter we have tried to answer some immediate questions that concern you. Next we will help you think about your options.

5

What Are My Options?

As a pregnant single, you will want to look at all the options available to you and your child. Each alternative is presented here briefly and then explored in more detail.

Do You Want to Be a Single Parent?

You can better understand the everyday realities of single parenting if you read material on this subject. Visit your library and ask one of the staff to help you locate books on this topic.

Most pregnancy care centers have group sessions for new and prospective single parents. Try to attend a few of their meetings. When you carefully listen to others share their joys, problems, and feelings, you can gain better perspectives. Other new mothers may present ideas, problems, or possibilities that you have not considered.

Do You Plan to Marry?

You and the father of your baby may have thought about marriage. If so, take note that many couples who feel they have to get married do not "live happily ever after."

"Teenage marriages have the highest rate of divorce." Over 50 percent of the girls who marry at age 15 to 19 get divorced. The divorce rate for parents who have their first child before they are 18 is three times greater than for parents who have their first child after age 20.[1]

However, maybe both of you consider yourselves ready to live by the marriage vows (see chapter 10). If so, you as a couple will gain benefits by seeking premarital counseling. If not, talk with a professional at any agency specifically designed to help you and your child.

Have You Considered Adoption?

Releasing your child for adoption may be a tough choice to consider. The birth father, and maybe your parents and his parents, should certainly be part of the counseling procedure for this issue.

It is extremely important that you seek up-to-date information about adoption and make a planned and unhurried decision.

Each of these three options is difficult, whether to be a single parent, to marry, or to let your baby be adopted. One won't be easier than the others.

Any decision you make will require a sacrifice. When you think about your options, remember to consider the welfare of everyone involved, including your child. Since the baby within you is part of God's good gift of life, it is wise to preserve that life out of respect for God and for your own emotional health. This effectively rules out abortion. In extreme situations of physical and emotional risk to the mother, competent counselors will help you weigh the options.

Thinking Things Through

Do you really have a choice? You may feel there is only one alternative for you. Not so! Allow yourself to brainstorm. The choices may not seem to fit you, but evaluate them anyway. You do have at least two choices: you can keep the baby, or you can place the baby for adoption.

We recommend that you set aside a period of time each week to concentrate on one option. Then spend an equal amount of time thinking about each of the other options.

Write down the pros and cons of each choice, what counts for it, and what counts against it. For each option, list the changes or plans you'd choose to make in your own life. A sample form is included on the next page.

Your final decision shouldn't be made until *after* the baby is born. However, it is best if you can come to a tentative conclusion two months before delivery. If you wait until the last minute, your feelings of the moment may take over and make the decision.

Do you know someone who's been in a similar situation? Maybe you think you should make the same choice she made. Remember that her decision was made on the basis of *her* circumstances. Your decision needs to be based on your own experiences and goals. Each of us is unique. It's important you make the choice right for *you.*

How can you make good choices? Where do you begin?

If you can view your problems more objectively, you will be equipped to make good decisions. The next chapter is designed to help you with the decision-making process.

Option 1		**Option 2**		**Option 3**	
Pros	*Cons*	*Pros*	*Cons*	*Pros*	*Cons*

6

How Do I Make Good Decisions?

NOW THERE ARE TWO LIVES for you to consider. The decisions you make in the next few months will affect both of you for the rest of your lives. Sound frightening? If your choices are based solely on feelings, they can be.

Look at decisions you've made in the past. Did you avoid the issues? Put them off? This is definitely one time that procrastinating won't be possible. You can wait for a few months, but not forever.

Maybe you're the kind of person who sifts through all the possibilities and then stands firm. Perhaps you're the kind who, on a whim, changes her mind from day to day.

It is dangerous to make decisions right away and then spend a lot of time justifying them. Some young women have tunnel vision. Their decisions are already made, and they refuse to look at the alternatives. Frequently, they change their decisions at the last minute.

The best choices are those that solve more problems than they create, those that agree best with your lifestyle.

Questions to Ask Yourself

- Am I impulsive?
- Must I have the solution right away?
- Am I impatient?

- Do I deal with the problem head-on?
- Do I avoid the issue?
- Do I blame others?
- Do I think people don't approve of anything I do?
- Do I let or expect others to make decisions for me?
- How much risk and uncertainty can I tolerate?
- Am I a perfectionist? Must everything be just right?
- Am I rather good at predicting outcomes?
- Am I an optimist, or a pessimist?

Answering these questions honestly will give you an idea of how you handle decision making. It is possible to make wise decisions if you know the steps to follow.

How to Make a Good Decision

1. Identify the problem.
2. List alternative courses of action.
3. Gather information helpful in reaching a decision.
4. Consider the consequences of each alternative.
5. Consider the risks in making this decision.
6. Study how your values help you make decisions and carry them out. What is most or less important to you?
7. Reach a conclusion you believe is best.

Your Situation Today

What would happen if you took no positive steps to decide what to do about your baby? Here is what happened to one young woman who did just that:

> Heather, age sixteen, realized she had missed periods, but she blamed it on being irregular. When she started to gain weight, she told herself she was eating too much ice cream. Heather found excuses to deny real-

ity and talked herself out of accepting the pregnancy as possible.

She kept going out with friends to dances, continued gymnastic lessons, and wore tight pants. Subconsciously she knew she was pregnant, but she wouldn't allow herself to think about the issue, much less discuss it.

Finally Heather's mother questioned her. Although Heather denied any problem, her mother suspected the truth and took her daughter to a pregnancy care center. One month later, Heather had the baby.

This denial made it extremely difficult for Heather. She had to make a hurried decision. She also had to catch up in dealing honestly with all the hormonal and emotional changes that occur during and after pregnancy.

As she lay in the hospital bed considering the two lives she was now responsible for, Heather had no information on which to base her decisions.

You, on the other hand, can take control of your situation right now. Think about some decisions you've made before. Which classes did you decide to take? Why? Did you choose to enroll in driver's education, or wait another year? What kind of summer jobs did you apply for? Why?

Did you take definite control, or did you just let events carry you along?

Pressures from Others

Will you make your decisions because you think it's what someone else wants you to do? Will you make your decisions based on your own thoughts and feelings?

Take a sheet of paper and list all the important people in your life. Beside each name write what each person thinks you should do and why. How important is this person's opinion to you?

The following story illustrates what can happen when a young woman takes the opinions of someone else as more important than her own.

> Rachel, age thirty and an independent career woman, was busy climbing the corporate ladder. She initially wanted to place her baby for adoption. Rachel felt unready to be a mother and had many personal goals left to fulfill.
>
> However, when she told her mother, who had seven children of her own, her mom exclaimed, "Oh, no! You can't give away my grandchild!" This thought stayed with Rachel throughout her pregnancy.
>
> Not having her mother's support was difficult. In fact, it was too tough. To please her mother, Rachel kept the baby.
>
> This decision divided the family because Rachel's father had a hard time accepting the circumstances.

Are You in Touch with Your Feelings?

Put your feet up. Sit back and daydream. What was life like one year ago? Did you have the same interests and activities then? Who were your friends back then? How did you spend your time? What was important to you? What were your goals?

Now move into the present. How has the picture changed? Do you feel any different? What is important to you now? What occupies most of your time? Who do you count as your friends today? What are your plans for the future?

Perhaps fifteen-year-old Jennifer's story will illustrate the changes that can take place in a year:

Twelve months ago, Jennifer was interested in Tom. Now she considers him immature, a loser. Jennifer used to collect slogan buttons, wear flamboyant hats, and enjoy wearing fake tattoo hearts on the side of her face. Her reading material consisted of romance stories. Looking back on these activities, she thinks to herself, *How infantile!*

Last year Jennifer wanted to be an airline stewardess. This year she seriously considered attending Julliard School of Music. Then she became pregnant. Obviously, her goals, if not completely changed, will at least need to be shelved for a while.

Jennifer has a lot of growing up to do. Many changes have occurred in her life as a result of turning fifteen and becoming pregnant. How she feels now, compared with how she'll feel at age twenty-one, is like comparing apples and bananas.

With a counselor's help, Jennifer can see that although she'll feel different at twenty-one, the decisions she makes today will forever affect her future.

Identifying Your Goals

What are your goals for education and a career? Have you thought about a vocational or technical school? Is it more realistic to study for your General Equivalency Diploma (GED)? Maybe you plan to attend college, or perhaps you are striving for an advancement in your present job.

What about a family? Do you want marriage? Children? Have you decided to remain single?

Have you thought about your goals for personal growth? Maybe you want to read fifty books a year, or travel to several cities or other countries. Would you choose to take swimming, tennis, racquetball, or aerobics classes?

You also need to look at your financial picture. Will your current income keep you and your baby above the poverty level? Will you be able to afford your own apartment or new furniture? What about a down payment on a home or a ten-acre farm?

How would the responsibilities of parenthood affect your pursuit of these objectives?

Outside Counseling

It helps to have an objective person guiding you through your decision-making process. Sometimes when we have difficult choices to make, we'd like to avoid the subject, as Heather did. Often another person can help us face the important issues.

There are people specially trained to help you make arrangements for your best possible care; they can help you prepare for the future. Local pregnancy care centers and agencies are available to help you. (See the back of this book.) You can get advice from these centers for little or no charge.

At these centers, you will find people who care about your well-being and that of your baby. They may be called counselors, advocates, or social workers. As you chat with a counselor, she will help you to talk your way through to good solutions.

With her care and concern, a counselor will give you the opportunity to take a look at your situation and the changes you want to make for a happier future. She can also help you gauge your readiness for parenting.

Here are remarks from young women who were helped by visiting with someone at a pregnancy care center:

Beth: The counselor was great. She was sensitive, yet helped me make my own decision without giving her opinion on what to do.

Jackie: My social worker was a real help. I didn't know where else to turn, but I came to her and found acceptance and support.

Ann: They had good suggestions. I like the way they took all the time necessary; I never felt rushed.

Denise: They supported me a great deal without being pushy or overbearing.

Laura: Instead of taking control of my life, the counselor allowed me to have control.

As these comments suggest, when you meet with a counselor, she can give you insight, provide a list of helpful resources, and lend you moral support. Just as important, she can serve as a mediator between you and your parents, or between you and your baby's father.

She can also counsel you about personal problems apart from plans for the baby. Depending on your needs, she can assist in obtaining financial aid, medical care, prenatal and childbirth education, and if necessary, housing, maternity clothes, and transportation.

On the next few pages are some activity sheets for you to complete. You may want to do them now, and then again with an objective and concerned counselor.

Help in Your Decision Making

The following list of words describes various kinds of feelings. Put an X beside the words that describe you when you think about releasing your baby for adoption. Circle the words that describe your feelings when you think about raising your child.

anxious	deserted	joyful
fearful	upset	depressed
excited	terrific	tense
elated	loving	free
happy	manipulated	unloving
lonely	content	sad
relieved	peaceful	mean
embarrassed	locked-in	fulfilled

You may also find it helpful to keep a diary or journal of your thoughts and feelings.

Make two lists: List all the problems you could have as you raise your baby. List all the problems that could arise if you release your baby for adoption. Think about living with one option, then about living with the other. Which can you live with the best?

Play the role of a young woman who wants to raise her baby. Write all the convincing reasons why this is the better alternative. Now pretend you are the young woman who wants to release her baby for adoption. Write all the reasons why this is the better choice.

Consider the Child

In making your decision, concentrate on what you want for your child—for emotional and physical needs, needed family relationships, education, and vocation.

Problems If	
I raise my baby—	I release my baby—

Reasons Why	
I want to raise my baby—	I want to release my baby—

Consider Yourself

Motherhood is an overwhelming responsibility at times. The next chapter will help you decide if *you* are prepared to be a mother.

7

Am I Ready for Motherhood?

YOU MAY REMEMBER YOUR MOTHER saying in an exasperated tone, "Just wait till you have children of your own!" Perhaps you tried to tease her out of whatever it was that made her angry. At the same time, you may have said, "Oh, that's light-years away!"

Neither you nor your mom realized how fast those "light-years" would pass. Let's take a look at the joys, hassles, and responsibilities of parenting.

Joys

If you have an older sister or girlfriend who's had a baby, you can remember the fascination and excitement of seeing the newborn for the first time. Before the baby was born, perhaps you went to the baby shower and took note of all the darling, tiny outfits. You saw the warm, happy glow on the expectant mother's face. All eyes were focused on her; she was in the "spotlight."

These are all pleasant and wonderful things, but they last only a short time. The spotlight soon dims. Then it's time to take the baby home from the hospital. There are many joys in being a mother. Yet the responsibility of caring for a new life is awesome. Many heartaches and headaches go with the title "Mom."

Lynn's Story

A young woman named Lynn found her child was very demanding. Because she lived with her parents, Lynn thought they would provide support. Instead, they offered their advice as the "only way" to raise the child.

She sadly recognized the negative effect this child sometimes had on her life. Her decision to keep the baby was made in haste. She often regretted it.

If Lynn had written all her needs out on paper, it might have looked like this:

Emotional: I need to be nurtured and loved. I need to have my self-esteem built up. I need to live in a secure environment and to be encouraged by my parents.

Physical: I need medical attention, food, a home in which to live, and clothes; I *want* the latest style.

Spiritual: I need church and Sunday school. We do worship as a family and even pray together.

On paper, this would look wonderful. But the reality was different. Lynn said, "I was put down a lot by my father. He just criticized me and didn't know how to compliment me. As for a secure environment, my parents picked at each other and seemed to thrive on bickering.

"Concerning physical affection, I don't remember hugs from either of them. Although we went to church, the lessons didn't carry over at home. I felt guilty about thinking they were hypocrites."

Lynn took a good look at her situation, plus the added responsibility of her new baby. She finally realized her decision to keep the child was negatively affecting her emotions and ultimately her entire life. However, no one could tell her this when she chose to keep her baby. Lynn had not realized that she would encounter so much stress.

Measure Your Stress

"Stress experts have come up with the Stress Index Chart. 'Life-change unit points' were assigned to typical life events. See for yourself where you stand. Add the points to get your score.

"If you score less than 150, you're doing well; between 150 and 300, you probably have too much stress in your life. And because stress causes physical illness, if you score over 300 points, it can mean you're headed for a major health change."[1]

What About You?

As the chart on the next page shows, definite adjustments are required in motherhood. The manner in which you handle these changes will depend on your physical and emotional health, and on the support you receive from family and concerned loved ones. Your own needs will be great, but you may find most of your attention focused on caring for your child. [2]

Your Child's Needs

Let's pretend that you can see into the future. What do you imagine as characteristics for your child at different ages? What will the child need? Include physical, emotional, social, spiritual, and educational needs.

The Stress of Adjusting to Change

Rank of Event		*Stress Points*
1.	Death of spouse	100
2.	Divorce	73
3.	Marital separation	65
4.	Jail term	63
5.	Death of close family member	63
6.	Personal injury or illness	53
7.	Marriage	50
8.	Fired from job	47
9.	Marital reconciliation	45
10.	Retirement	45
11.	Health change of family member	44
12.	Pregnancy	40
13.	Sexual difficulties	39
14.	Gain of new family member	39
15.	Business readjustment	39
16.	Change in financial state	38
17.	Death of close friend	36
18.	Change of work	36
19.	More or fewer marital arguments	35
20.	Mortgage over $10,000	31
21.	Foreclosure of mortgage or loan	30
22.	Change in responsibility at work	29
23.	Son or daughter leaving home	29
24.	Trouble with in-laws	29
25.	Outstanding personal achievement	28
26.	Spouse begins or stops work	26
27.	Beginning or end of school	26
28.	Change in living conditions	25

29.	Revision of personal habits	24
30.	Trouble with boss	23
31.	Change in work hours/conditions	20
32.	Change in residence	20
33.	Change in schools	20
34.	Change in recreation	19
35.	Change in church activities	19
36.	Change in social activities	18
37.	Mortgage or loan less than $10,000	17
38.	Change in sleeping habits	16
39.	More or fewer family get-togethers	15
40.	Change in eating habits	15
41.	Vacation	13
42.	Christmas	12
43.	Minor violations of the law	11

Imagine Yourself as a Parent

What do you think parenting will be like? Do you feel it will mean having someone always there to love you? Are you excited when you imagine experiencing the dramatic way a child grows? Will parenting give purpose to your life?

If your child disobeys or throws a tantrum, will you be able to apply discipline? Do you imagine you will lose a lot of freedom? Will you feel trapped?

These questions point out the appealing *and* unappealing aspects of parenting.

What My Child Will Be Like at—	What My Child Will Need at This Age—
Birth	*Needs*
Six years old	*Needs*
Twelve years old	*Needs*
Fifteen years old	*Needs*
Nineteen years old	*Needs*

Appealing and Unappealing

In the first column, list the things you are looking forward to in raising your baby. In the second, list what you don't look forward to. This may be difficult. Think back to some of the experiences your parents had with you as you were growing up.

Your relationship with your child may differ, but there are no "perfect" parent-child relationships. There are happy and sad occasions in all families.

Appealing	**Unappealing**

Now that you have looked at some of the positive and negative features of raising a child, you realize that there will be inevitable adjustments. You don't want to have a lot of distasteful surprises down the road. Ask yourself the following questions, and write your answers on a separate sheet of paper.

A Change for the Better?

• What do I want out of life for myself? What do I think is important?

• How will a child interfere with my growth and development?

• Can I handle a child and a job or school at the same time?

• Will my child change my educational plans?

- Can I afford to support a child?
- Do I want to raise a child in my neighborhood, or will I be financially able to move?
- Am I ready to give up my freedom to do what I want to do when I want to do it?
- Am I willing to give at least eighteen years of my life to being responsible for a child's well-being?

After pondering these questions, you can understand some of the changes that will occur in your lifestyle. You may be better able to relate to the following story:

A Definite Change in Jan's Lifestyle

Jan was used to getting up at 6:30, eating a light breakfast of toast and apple juice, or sometimes nothing at all, and then going off to work at the drugstore. She sometimes resented her low-paying job. As a school dropout, she knew she couldn't do much better until she got her GED. Her life was fairly predictable and routine. Then it changed.

"I couldn't believe all the adjustments I had to make when I brought Susie home from the hospital," Jan said. "Thanks to my parents' willingness to baby-sit, I still worked at the drugstore. But my sleep patterns sure got weird! Two o'clock in the morning is not exactly my shining hour.

"Susie is a good baby—no colic or anything like that. But for one so tiny, she sure wears me out! It was my choice to raise her, and I'm not sorry. But I never knew I would be so tired! I'm learning fast about the 'joys of motherhood.' No matter what, though, I'm determined to be a good parent."

Types of Parents

Parents come in all sizes, shapes, and personalities. You have probably encountered friends whose parents treated them quite differently from the way your parents treated you. Some parents are lenient, others strict. Some are active, fun-loving parents, while some seem old and tired all the time. Some are generous, others frugal.

Sally's parents attended every musical, sports, or dramatic event when she took part. Betty's parents never seemed to care whether she was even in school. They were too involved in their own problems.

Reflect on the kinds of parents you've met. Ask yourself what kind of parent you will be. Consider these questions:

Am I Ready to Parent?

- Do I like children? What kind of experience have I had with them?
- Do I communicate easily?
- How do I express affection?
- Will I have enough patience to raise a child?
- Can I tolerate noise and confusion?
- Can I handle disrupted schedules?
- How do I release my anger? If I lost my temper, is it possible that I might abuse my child?
- What does discipline mean?
- Can I set limits, yet give some freedom?
- Do I want a perfect child?
- How do I get along with my parents?
- What will I do to avoid mistakes my parents made?
- Do I enjoy the activities children can do?
- Do I expect my child to achieve things I didn't achieve?

- Will I want my child to keep me from being lonely in my old age?
- By having a child, will I show others how mature I am?
- Do I expect my child to make my life happy?

Help! I Need Somebody!

If you decide to keep your baby, you are putting *yourself* on the line to do the major work of providing care. When those closest to you are available and give you loving support, that can add happiness to your life.

As an unmarried mother, you are going to want more than a *little* help from your friends and family. Figure out what support will really be available when you bring your baby home. Many friends have good intentions. However, often those intentions never become reality because of other obligations or loss of focus.

One unwed mother asked her closest friends what each would do to help her. Some of them made halfhearted efforts to help. Only one out of nine friends came through and did exactly what she had promised.

Think of some ways relatives and friends can help you. Consider things like babysitting, helping with laundry, shopping for groceries, figuring finances, or just providing friendship. List people who will accept and help you and your baby. After each name, describe the way each person could help. Who can you count on to do what?

Friend	Type of Help	How Reliable?

Make Room for Baby

A baby, *your* baby—a tiny bundle of flesh and bone—is a miniature human life. Although your baby is so small, she or he needs many things to make life comfortable. This section is designed to help you make room for baby.

Questions to Consider

1. What do I need in a layette? Where do I get it?
2. How many diapers and how much formula will I need in a week?
3. How much money do I need to supply my baby's necessities?
4. What baby furniture do I need? How can I get it?
5. Who will take care of my baby when I'm in school or at work?

6. How much does daycare cost? What will it provide?

7. Who will furnish medical care for my baby? What kind of care will the baby need?

8. How many hours can I spend each day with my baby?

Where Will We Live?

Where you live will depend on your age and family support. Some young women choose to live away from their parents. Because they become mothers themselves, they think it is best to live elsewhere. Two mothers in the same home can seem like one too many.

Mary decided to move out of her parents' home. She was eighteen and had recently delivered her baby. These are some of the questions she needed to answer:

- What is my source of income?
- How much can I afford for an apartment?
- How will I find one?
- What furniture will I need, and how do I obtain it?
- What else will I need for the apartment?
- How much money will I need each week to supply my personal needs?
- How much can I afford for utilities?

Mary had a lot to think about. You will too. It's better to try to answer these questions now. You don't want to be unprepared at the last minute.

On the other hand, many young women choose to remain at home. Cathy wanted to stay in her parents' house so she could finish her last year of high school. Cathy also had three brothers and sisters who lived at home. In planning for the baby, she had many things to discuss with her family:

• In what part of the house will Cathy and the baby stay?

• How do the rest of her family feel about her and the baby?

• What are potential areas of conflict? How can they be resolved?

• How can Cathy contribute to the monthly household expenses?

• Is Cathy expected to pay rent and help with the baby's expenses?

• How will her family participate in the care of the baby?

• Can she expect free babysitting services? What about laundry? Who will feed and change the baby?

• How will Cathy feel when other members of the family discipline her child?

• What about her situation in terms of dating, curfew, and personal freedom?

• Will Cathy's living arrangements meet her own needs for both structure and freedom?

The questions that Mary and Cathy had to deal with may overwhelm you. However, if you choose to raise your baby, they must be answered. Providing for a child is expensive. Our next chapter will help you to determine the costs of this challenge.

8

Money Matters

VANESSA O'CONNELL SAYS, "Families with annual household incomes of more than $55,000 spend, on average, $10,510 a year on their child during the first two years of life. You may end up spending more or less than the average—depending on where you live and whether you have other children—but the important thing is to be aware of upcoming expenses and budget for them.

"Diapers: A one-year supply of cloth diapers from a diaper service costs approximately $675, compared to about $360 for a year's supply of 2,600 disposables."[1]

Maybe you don't expect to use disposable diapers or organized daycare. That far-off time is hard to imagine when your baby isn't born yet. But if you choose to raise your child, you must consider financial matters.

In your opinion, which of the following are necessary and which are optional? Circle the necessary ones.

Apartment: rent, deposit	Electricity, deposit
Phone and deposit	Clothing for self
Clothing for baby	Food for self
Food for baby	Eating out
Recreation/social life	Health insurance
Transportation	Car insurance
Savings	Personal needs
Medical (eyeglasses, etc.)	Childcare
Gifts	Church

What Is All This Going to Cost Me?

Sarah, aged nineteen, had a good job at the telephone company. During her pregnancy, she lived at home. In her fifth month, she decided to move out after her baby was born.

With Mrs. Adams, her counselor at a pregnancy care center, Sarah took a good look at all that moving involved. First, the counselor advised Sarah to look through newspaper want ads, call rental agencies, talk to people at her church, and pick up apartment guides at the bank.

"I'm so thankful my counselor was there to help me sort through my living arrangements. In looking for housing, she suggested places I wouldn't have known or thought about," Sarah said.

Next, after Sarah had looked at several possibilities, she and Mrs. Adams listed locations and what each would cost. Seen on paper, it was much easier to choose where the best place would be for Sarah to live with her baby.

"After I made my decision to move into a cute little apartment not far from my work, my counselor talked with me about furniture for my apartment."

"Sarah, it's important to think about the kind of furnishings you need for yourself and the baby," Mrs. Adams said. She suggested that Sarah visit Salvation Army Thrift Stores, Goodwill Stores, and garage sales for good baby items. In addition, Sarah could ask her friends and relatives if they had items to loan or give to her.

Sarah skimmed newspaper advertisements for furniture store sales and carefully read the classified ads for bargains in kitchen equipment and linens.

"Then my counselor discussed the cost of utilities with me," Sarah remembered. "Mrs. Adams suggested I call and find out the cost of having a phone installed, what the monthly costs are, and what kind of deposit they wanted. I did the same thing with the electric company, asking for an estimate of monthly charges, their hookup fee, and the deposit required on my one-bedroom apartment.

"Our next topic was food and clothing costs. Mrs. Adams told me that getting all this stuff down on paper would help me budget my money better." Her counselor helped her estimate the monthly food bills. Sarah planned to breast-feed her baby, so the cost of infant formula wasn't included for the first several months.

"I needed to think about what clothes in my wardrobe would have to be replaced in the next six months and budget money for that," Sarah explained. "Mrs. Adams also gave me a list of nursery and layette items, then helped me write a list of what I needed."

Layette and Nursery Needs

Clothing

2 dozen cloth diapers *or*
2 packages disposable diapers
3-5 sleepers
3-5 receiving blankets
4 waterproof panties (with cloth diapers)
8 safety pins, double-locking heads (for cloth diapers)
Sweater set
6 cotton shirts
2 blanket sleepers
Booties and socks

Feeding Equipment

If breast-feeding, 2 or more bottles for water and juice
If bottle-feeding, 8 bottles, 8 nipples, 8 caps
Bottle and nipple brushes
Pre-sterilized, disposable nurser kit
4 bibs

Bed and Bath

2-3 crib blankets
3 fitted sheets
1 small waterproof pad
Bathinette or portable baby bath
Toiletries: soap or liquid cleanser, lotion, powder, cotton swabs, cream, petroleum jelly, moist towelettes, shampoo, ointment

For Outings

Bunting or pram suit
Insulated bottle and diaper bag
Stroller
Car seat

Basic Nursery Needs

Crib
Mattress
Crib bumper
Chest of drawers
Dressing or changing table
Rectal thermometers
Infant seat
Diaper pail
Record book
Nursery lamp
Crib mobile
Toys

Later Additions

Playpen and pad
Table and chair set
Safety gates and latches
Portable baby swing
Baby walker, jumper, or exerciser
Toy box
Portable stroller
Children's books
Toilet seat/chair

Medical Care

After attending her baby shower and buying a few new things, Sarah went to the same places she had explored for her furniture.

"With food, housing, and clothes out of the way, I had to think about my baby's medical needs," Sarah said. "Mrs.

Adams recommended that I read some books on this subject, then write down the medical care my baby would need for the first six months.

"This included making a call to my local public health office to find out about immunization schedules, locations, and costs for a baby." She also called her family doctor's office to ask about costs for well-baby care in the first six months.

"Naturally, I talked with my health insurance company to find out what kind of coverage my baby and I had, and to see what else they had available," Sarah stressed. "After getting that information, I was better able to estimate my medical expenses and what would or wouldn't be covered each month.

"My personal needs were easier to list because I had already started to keep track about three months ago. I kept a pretty thorough rundown of items like toilet paper, aspirin, perfume, tampons, toothpaste, and cosmetics.

"It didn't take long to fill out this sheet my counselor gave me."

My Personal Needs	What They Cost

Sarah thought about another part of child rearing. Who would care for her baby while she worked? Sarah learned that she needed to check the costs at various local daycare centers and find out exactly what they provided.

She found some in the telephone book and newspaper ads and went to visit them. Her counselor told Sarah it would also be wise to ask some of her friends and relatives for hourly babysitting rates that they earned or paid.

The last item they discussed was transportation. Mrs. Adams asked Sarah to estimate her cost for transportation per month, then to consider available alternatives, such as mass transit.

The counselor finally gave Sarah a budget exercise sheet to fill out. "It was a pain to do," Sarah explained, "but it did help me see where my money would go each month."

We have included an exercise sheet here for you to complete. If you can get some idea now of what you'll need to purchase each month, later it won't be such a shock. More important, you'll have time to shop carefully and to prepare for expenses.

Keep in mind that the time you spend estimating your budget will be worth it. Writing the figures down now will save you money and many headaches later.

TANF and WIC

Help is available through the U.S. Department of Human Services with a program known as Temporary Assistance for Needy Families (TANF). States and provinces may use other names for such aid.

If you ask TANF for help, the agency will insist that you identify the father of your baby. When the father is legally identified, he will have responsibilities and rights.

Where Does All the Money Go?

Necessary Expenditures	Monthly Costs

Total __________

Optional Expenditures	Monthly Costs

Total __________

Monthly Income __________

Subtract Total of Necessary Items __________

Subtract Optional Items __________

Balance __________

The Women and Infant Care (WIC) program is designed to help improve the diet of pregnant women because the unborn baby is fed through the mother's body. When a woman participates in the WIC program, she learns which foods will help her have a healthy baby. She also can receive many of these foods at no cost.

To receive WIC benefits, the woman must have a health need that nutrition, education, and WIC foods can help. Needs are determined by medical history and family income.

As of July 1, 1997, there have been major changes in public assistance. To find out if you qualify, call your local health and human services department.

If you want to continue your education or pursue job training, TANF may be able to assist you with financing childcare. Many young, unwed mothers find they need financial help. In one southern county, over 70 percent of welfare recipients were teens when they bore their first child.

While it can be expensive to raise a child, it can also be rewarding. The next chapter will introduce you to four young women. Each looked for different "rewards" in motherhood.

9

Checking My Motives

UNWED MOTHERS HAVE VARIOUS reasons for deciding to keep and raise their children. Now is a good time to examine your motives. See if you can identify with any of these young women.

Kelly

Kelly, aged seventeen, expected her child to fulfill her own desperate need to be loved. "When I was thirteen, my father left us. Mom had to hold down two jobs to support my two sisters and me. She didn't have much time left over for affection."

This was Kelly's second pregnancy. After she placed her first baby for adoption, she suffered from a sense of loss and loneliness.

"When I got pregnant this time, I thought now I'd have someone to really love and someone who will love me. I believed I was ready to have another one, settle down, and make a good home. I felt the baby could give me just what I needed.

"The first six weeks with my son were okay. My mom would come over, and all my friends wanted to see the baby and hold him. The newness of it all was exciting! For the first time, I found a purpose in life and really thought someone needed me. All my life I just wanted to be needed."

Kelly's son is now two years old. "I do love him, but I'm finding out it's more than a give-and-take situation. I'm giving, giving, giving, and he's taking, taking, taking. Sometimes I feel drained, with no energy left and little love to give.

"At times he is quite demanding. I'll never forget the last time we went to the grocery store. What a scene! My son stood in the aisle with three bags of candy in his arms. One bag was halfway open, and he refused to let go. I stood there, afraid to take the bags away for fear he'd have a screaming tantrum. How embarrassing! I ended up buying all three bags.

"I recognize that my child's needs are important. But it's hard to be loving and to give of myself when I got so little attention in my younger years. There's so much I need for *me*. I know he needs discipline, activities to keep him busy, and loving attention. But it is an endless effort, and I have nothing left for myself."

Kelly looked reflective. "It's real nice when he's sitting in my lap. We cuddle together and rock in the chair. But sometimes he grabs my lipstick when I'm not looking and smears it on the wall. Then it's not so nice."

Carol

Carol is a mature nineteen-year-old who was brought up in a positive, loving family environment. "My reason for keeping the baby is that I felt I could parent her responsibly. I wanted to be the one to help my child develop physically, emotionally, and spiritually. I also wanted to work hard toward her overall well-being."

She is realistic and recognizes that there will be ups as well as downs with the responsibility of motherhood.

Carol is emotionally mature enough not to depend on the child to make her life happy.

"My own needs are being met through a great family support system. My baby's father is no longer involved, but I have a strong faith in God and can rely on God rather than on myself," she said. "I am highly motivated to parent. One thing that really helped me was to read some good books on childcare and parenting."

Her motive was basically good. She felt she could be a good parent, and she had the self-confidence to carry this out. She knew she could give to her baby and didn't need to receive a lot from her baby. Carol has a good self-image. Her strength comes from within, and she also relies on God's power to help her.

Ann

Ann felt trapped. "He's my child, and no one else is going to raise him. I got myself into this, so now I'll just have to suffer." Her family had told her repeatedly, "You must keep your child. There's no other way!"

The neighbor lady had placed her baby for adoption. When Ann's mother heard this, she was horrified: "How in the world could she just up and give away her little baby!"

She got the message. According to her mother, adoption was not the thing to do. Her cultural background said, "You don't give away your own flesh and blood. It's taboo."

She believed the only option was to keep the baby. Her values suggested she was good if she kept the baby, but bad if she released him. As a result, her goals and ambitions were put on hold.

Before long Ann developed resentment toward the

whole situation: "My family is well-off and has promised to provide the finances, but I feel locked in, like this is my lot in life.

"I'm graduating in a couple months and would love to go on to college, to be free and do what I want to do. But that's out for a while. I guess I decided to keep the baby because I never saw any other choice."

Ellen

Ellen based her decision to keep the child on a sincere hope that the baby would force the baby's father to continue their relationship. "I believed that once Charlie watched me go through childbirth and actually saw the baby, he would realize my love for him and give me what I wanted, a wedding. I counted on the delivery room experience to convince him that we should marry.

"I was stunned when he still wanted me to place the baby for adoption. He said he didn't feel we were financially ready. Charlie didn't want to think about settling down or handling the responsibility. He said we'd get married later. That was hard to take. I felt like telling him he could either take the baby and me now or forget it. His attitude was like a slap in the face. I just couldn't understand how he would want to continue our relationship, yet not include our baby."

Ellen never told Charlie that she'd made a decision. "I know how badly he wanted me to let the baby be adopted. But I thought he wouldn't be able to resist his own son. So I kept quiet and hoped he'd change his mind," Ellen stated.

"A couple days after the birth, Charlie came to see me at the hospital. My parents told him about my decision. He didn't show any emotion, but I sensed he was upset.

"After my folks left, Charlie really let me have it! 'Ellen, I've told you over and over from the very beginning! Can't you get it through your head? I will not marry you if you keep that kid!' With that, he stomped out of my hospital room.

"Although he'd made it clear where he stood, I refused to give up hope," Ellen said. "After I took the baby home, I figured when he came to visit me, he'd have to see the baby, too. Then he'd understand that I was being a good mother to his son. He'd see me hold our baby and watch me take care of him. I was determined to prove to him that I could be not only a good mother, but also a good wife."

You may have the same motives that Ellen had, or maybe you identify with Kelly, Carol, or Ann. The next chapter will help you test your readiness for marriage and give you guidelines to prepare yourself for the big walk down the aisle.

10

Will I Say "I Do"?

MARRIAGE OFTEN SEEMS LIKE the best solution to the problem pregnancy, the easiest way out. Your womanly instincts may tell you that babies belong within the holy bonds of matrimony. Perhaps you think it wouldn't look right without a father around the house.

Gossip about you may pressure you to marry. Don't let tongue-waggers make your decision for you.

On the other hand, if you are ready to settle down, this alternative can be wonderful for all concerned. However, it takes two committed people to make it work.

Marriage is a commitment to a stable union, a lasting relationship between a woman and a man. As two people become a family, each can experience personal growth, joy, and satisfaction while working things out together.

Let's see what you need to make this solution work. Such exploring will help you determine whether or not your relationship has what it takes to make it last.

Is He Your Prince Charming?

Have you ever dreamed about the best time to marry and the perfect person with whom to settle down and start a family? When is that ideal time? What would the father of your baby be like?

Theresa shared with a support group of pregnant

women. She had always dreamed of beginning her family after she and her husband had some time to "just be together and get to know each other."

"I never really wanted to get married until my late twenties," Theresa said. "I wanted to experience and savor life before settling down." She shared dreams of travel to Europe, then of time spent raising her horses, which she had entered in shows for several years.

However, the truth is that she is seventeen and pregnant, and the boy she has dated for the past five months wants to marry her.

Theresa's dreams contrast sharply with her current situation. "After thinking it through, I feel I can sacrifice my 'ideal' and commit myself instead to raising my child," she said. "My dreams of travel and horses will have to wait. What still concerns me, though, is whether I want to work at being Steve's wife for the rest of my life."

Steve doesn't have all the qualities she looks for in a husband. He *is* the father of her child. Still, she wonders if she can give up the hope of marrying her dream man.

Which Qualities Are Important?

Theresa felt that the most important thing she wanted in her husband was the ability to gather wealth. "Steve makes five dollars an hour right now. He assures me that with raises over the next few years, his pay will be sufficient.

"I guess I was looking for more than just 'sufficient.' I want a large house in the country, a three-car garage, and a car in each stall. My dreams include a cook and a live-in nanny. Oh, well," she sighed. "I've always heard that money doesn't buy happiness. Now I'll have a chance to find out if that's true."

The next item Theresa looked for in a man was personality. "Steve is loaded with pizzazz and has a terrific sense of humor. He's the type of person who makes you feel good just to be around him. Everybody gets depressed once in a while, but he hasn't got time for that sad-faced stuff. He's too busy enjoying life and all it has to offer."

Thus on personal attraction and human warmth, Steve and Theresa have much going for them.

Her man's faith was important to Theresa. "I never cared much for people who were wishy-washy about what they believe," she said. "Steve is wonderful in that department! He believes there is a God, and we've spent many hours discussing how good our Creator is.

"Sometimes we visit my church; other times we go to his. Our beliefs match perfectly, so we wouldn't have trouble in this area."

Think It Through

Here's an exercise to help you weigh the question of marriage. Fill in blanks for each.

Qualities of Current Boyfriend	**Qualities of Ideal Mate**

How do the lists compare? What qualities are lacking? Can you overlook these?

What Is Your Relationship Like?

Keys to successful marriage are *love* and *commitment.* Do you really love the man you are thinking of marrying? Does he love you? "Of course!" you say. But are you sure? Would you stick together no matter what?

Sometimes love is hard to define and recognize. The true measure of love comes when you, as a couple, are faced with everyday problems of life together.

Believe it or not, the time will come when the tingling stops. There can be sweet interludes, but it won't always be moonbeams and roses. H. Norman Wright, author of thirty-six books on marriage, says, "Most people prepare more for their driver's test than they do for marriage."

To help you prepare, consider the following questions:

1. If I weren't pregnant, would I still think of my boyfriend as a possible marriage partner?
2. Do my boyfriend and I understand each other's feelings about religion, work, family, raising children, and goals for life? Are these feelings compatible? Do they support good parenting?
3. Is sex the focal point of our relationship? Do we share more than physical attraction?
4. Do we have common interests and hobbies?
5. How well do we communicate with each other?
6. What attracts us to each other?
7. What are his faults and shortcomings? Can I accept these?
8. How much concern does he seem to have about the baby?

9. Do both of us feel the same way about wanting to parent the child?

10. How would my boyfriend contribute to childcare responsibilities?

11. How stable is our relationship?

12. How do I really feel about marriage being a commitment for life?

13. Will we be able to share each other unselfishly with our child?

14. Are we *both* ready to give our time and energy to raising our baby?

Heavy questions, right? But they do need to be answered, especially if you're serious about marriage.

Even when a couple enters into marriage without a child to consider, there's a big adjustment to make.

Marriage Is an Adjustment

Let's return to Theresa's story. "My .counselor really helped me see some things I hadn't thought about before. She told me, 'There are three major transitions in the lives of most people. They are changes from

- adolescence to adulthood.
- single life to married life.
- non-parenthood to parenthood.'

"Then my counselor explained, 'Each transition takes time. You need to complete one change before moving on to the next one. If you get pregnant and married while you are in your teens, you are forced to make the transitions all at once.'

"What she said made me realize that marriage to Steve is more than slipping rings on our fingers and calling ourselves man and wife. After the honeymoon, there would be big adjustments to make. And they'd be ones we would have to make together, both of us going through them at exactly the same time.

"After we discussed some adjustments and changes that were bound to happen, my counselor gave me two copies of a stress chart [see chapter 7]. She told Steve and me each to put a star by the ones that affected us. It was a painful eye-opener! Neither one of us could have guessed we'd each rack up close to three hundred points of stress!

"The next time I met with my counselor," Theresa said, "she suggested we talk about why I wanted to get married. Most people don't consciously think about their reasons for wanting a wedding. In my situation, with the baby coming and all, it was quite helpful to put my motives into words."

Have You Faced Your Aims?

Have you thought about *why* you want to get married? Is it an escape? Do you feel it will get you out of a poor family environment? Will marriage give you a chance to develop the stable family you've longed for? Remember, over 50 percent of girls who marry at age 15 to 19 get divorced.

Perhaps you want marriage so someone will be there to care for you and love you. The truth is that we all *first* have to find and love ourselves *before* we can love others. We take ourselves with us wherever we go.

Maybe you haven't made much progress in loving yourself. Marriage can add to your confusion if you are still trying to discover who you are and who you want to become. This can be worse than taking a double course load at school.

On the other hand, you may have been in a relationship for years. Neither one of you are kids anymore. Now that you're pregnant, you believe the two of you will marry.

Does your boyfriend agree with this? Will you marry out of guilt? Do you think marriage is the only honorable and legal choice? Is this what you're *expected* to do?

Many couples who follow this line of reasoning feel trapped in their marriages. The trapped feeling can lead to anger and resentment toward the spouse. Both partners can feel a sincere sense of responsibility, yet have an underlying hostile attitude.

Then the baby might become an object of resentment, even physical abuse. If *you* grew up in an angry atmosphere, there is a greater chance that you will abuse your child. Most of us tend to parent the way we've been parented. In spite of that, as parents, we are still responsible for what we do.

Perhaps your parents are pressuring you to marry. A generation ago, when a woman became pregnant before marriage, the two were honor bound to say, "I do." A lot of these hastily arranged marriages did not result in living happily ever after. Instead, both people felt trapped. Some couples today feel trapped.

Your parents may be urging you to "make it legal," to "give the baby a name." In all honesty, however, the opinions of friends and relatives are far less important than the marriage's stability—or lack of it. A bad marriage would be harmful to your baby, your husband, and you.

If you plan to marry, what do you expect to get out of it?

Your Marriage Expectations

Remember the movie *Blue Hawaii,* starring Elvis Presley? In one scene he and his beautiful costar float on a gorgeous flower-bedecked boat. That will remain one of the most romantic wedding sequences on film.

The media are filled with fantasies of roses, orange blossoms, and moonlit nights. Such stories hide the thorns and thunderstorms. The movie producers go to extraordinary lengths to portray love and marriage as something magic and mystical.

People say, "Where love is blind, marriage is a great eye-opener." Some of us have been there, in a less-than-perfect marriage. We recommend that couples open their eyes wide *before* entering marriage. You need to talk things over.

How do you feel about *roles* in marriage? Are you for the traditional division of tasks, with the husband bringing home the food and you preparing it? Do you steer toward the more modern patterns of sharing financial and housekeeping responsibilities?

Discuss partners' roles and tasks with your boyfriend. You may find you are in absolute agreement. More likely, you will need to compromise.

Do you foresee any *obstacles* to the two of you marrying? What happens if both of your families are cool to the idea? Is there a problem with finances? Maybe both of you are underage. What then? Are you and your boyfriend able to handle the loss of cherished goals? Is yours a stable relationship? Do either of you feel forced into marriage? These are questions that need to be voiced openly and discussed *now*.

What *benefits* will marriage provide? Do you really believe that three can live as cheaply as one? You would have companionship and never have to worry about a date. You'd have a father for the child, and a husband to help provide for the three of you.

If the benefits outweigh the obstacles, then marriage could be tailor-made for you. Remember that marriage should solve more problems than it creates.

Maybe you're not 100 percent in agreement with marriage to your baby's father. In that case, your next step is to consider adoption.

11

Making Plans for Adoption

IF YOU ARE EIGHTEEN OR OLDER, the decision about whether to place your baby for adoption must be made by you and by the legally recognized baby's father, if he is eighteen or older. That decision does not belong to your parents, your friends, a counselor, an agency, or the court, though they will help you sort out what is involved. If you or the father is under eighteen, your parents or his parents must sign the adoption papers.

If you are an adult, no one can force you to release your child against your will, unless there is evidence that you have mistreated your child. You have the first right to parent your child.

This is the legal situation in most states and provinces, but laws for your area may vary. For local information, ask your counselor or an attorney specializing in adoptions.

To make an intelligent decision, look at all the options, including the tough choice of adoption. Let's listen as Holly tells her story.

Holly's Unguarded Moment

How can I describe Bob Avalon? Weird. When spitballs sailed through the air in our classroom, they usually came from Bob.

"Don't think I didn't see that!" our teacher announced.

"Try that one more time, and I promise you two hours of detention." Besides being our class clown, Bob played center for our Calvary Christian School basketball team. As captain of the cheerleading squad, it was hard for me not to notice him.

"Hi ya, Holl," Bob called out at school or at games. "How's it goin'?"

Each time I talked with him, Bob's electrifying smile made me think he wasn't so weird after all.

Soon he started walking me to classes. One day he asked, "I'd like to carry your books. Can I?"

"No way," I retorted. "That's dumb."

My remark didn't seem to embarrass him. He still walked with me each day.

As our friendship deepened, my image of Bob as top spitball champ faded. Instead, I saw him as a kind, courteous, and caring person. Weeks passed, and we discovered we had a lot in common. Both of us enjoyed nature, long country walks, burgers and fries, some of the same books, and funny television programs.

Those were good times, happy times, and our romance grew. After four months, our dream romance turned into disaster.

One weekend, while I baby-sat two children overnight at their home, Bob decided to join me. He told his parents he was going to camp out with friends.

At first we only watched TV and talked. But it wasn't long before I heard myself whisper, "Bob, this is all wrong."

"Yeah, I know," he murmured, "but God will forgive us."

I never should have listened to him. The next day I felt dirty and full of guilt. I sensed that what we'd done signaled the beginning of the end of our relationship.

About a month later, my body began to change. Angry, hurt, and bitter, I felt rebellious against everybody, including the Lord.

"Why, God? How could you let this happen to me?" I moaned. "I've always been a pretty good kid. Now this! Why?"

Confessing to my mom was tough. She took the news hard, yet remained supportive, and took me to our family doctor. Within an hour after Doctor Berg examined me, the nurse announced, "The test is positive. You'll be a mom in eight months."

She might as well have said I was going to *die* in eight months. That's exactly how I felt. I cried all the way home.

My first thought was abortion. The second idea was suicide. Neither was a real option for me. I loved the Lord and knew that his creation of life was good.

After a few hours of self-pity, I asked God to forgive my lapse of judgment. I also asked forgiveness for my earlier attitude toward God. Why blame God for *my* sin? Then I begged the Lord to walk me through this crisis.

When I saw Bob the next day, I decided to be blunt. "You're going to find this hard to believe, but I'm pregnant."

"Ah, come off it, honey. Don't tease me that way." He laughed. But he immediately saw by the look on my face that I wasn't joking. His next words surprised me. "Well, I guess we'll have to get married."

I couldn't believe it. Here we were, two teenagers, and he was talking *marriage!* I sure didn't want that.

"No, I'm afraid not," I stated firmly. "There is no way I'd get married now."

We parted then and walked off in opposite directions.

After my church family found out, they lovingly supported me. In fact, over the months, at least five women came to me and confessed through tears that they were pregnant before marriage. People sent kind notes, expressing their prayers for me and asking the Lord to show me the right way to go.

Through most of my pregnancy, I felt that keeping the baby was the right way to go. I prayed for Jesus to help me to be a good mother. In my eighth month, I visited a Christian social worker my pastor recommended.

At the pregnancy care center, Nancy made me take a realistic look at the cost in time, energy, and money needed to raise a child. At first I resented her presenting these facts to me. Up until we talked, I dreamily thought, *Somehow, someway, my baby and I will manage.*

I went home that night disturbed by all she had said. At three in the morning, I awoke, and I couldn't get back to sleep. I prayed again about the tiny life within me. Then I pictured the joy my baby could bring a childless couple.

I tossed and turned with images of my happy child in a Christian home with two parents. Just before daybreak, with the Lord's help, I decided to place my baby for adoption. At once, peace surrounded me, and I fell into a sound sleep.

During my pregnancy, whenever I was anxious and fearful, I played praise songs on the piano or escaped to my room for quiet times reading the Word. Psalm 139:13-16 comforted me tremendously.

In this passage, the psalmist acknowledges that God created his inner parts and knit them together wonderfully in his mother's womb. He also praises God for knowing him and his future days even before one of them came into existence. I knew these verses talked about *both* my baby and me. In the last month of my pregnancy, God gave me an extra measure of tranquillity.

One night I realized it was time. After a short labor in a small birthing room of a large hospital, I delivered a healthy baby boy. As I held and fed him, I stared, overwhelmed at this precious gift of life. Ten fingers, ten toes, all the right parts, plus cherub cheeks. A perfect infant!

I would miss my baby and grieve for him. Yet God gave me comfort by helping me focus on the happy parents who had waited so long for a child.

As I look back, I thank the Lord for his care for me at all times, his gentle guidance, and his reassurance that I was his child. My remorse for one wrong act of passion paved the way for his healing oil of love to work in my life.

I am not happy that I disobeyed God, but I'm more than thankful that he forgave and helped me deal with the consequences of my unguarded moment.[1]

Natural Instincts

God gave most women a natural maternal instinct. You will be keenly aware of this as you carry your child. This instinct also helps you want to put the baby's best interests before your own.

If you decide to place your baby for adoption, please be aware that *many* childless couples are praying to be blessed with a child. Today, couples waiting for children far outnumber the babies available.

Reasons to Place for Adoption

At age nineteen, Trudy lived in a sparsely furnished, basement efficiency apartment with her two children. One day she called the Child Protection Agency. Her eighteen-month-old had upset her, and Trudy was afraid she would lose control.

Trudy had many emotional needs herself, such as a big desire to be loved and accepted. Her relationships with men had not been positive. Trudy admitted that most of the reason for her anger and hot temper was because she was always trying to please others, never herself.

She had a host of hostile feelings toward her newborn's father, who was not the father of her toddler. Her call to the Child Protection Agency arose out of deep concern for the welfare—even for the life—of her ten-day-old baby.

"I've made so many mistakes with the first child," Trudy mourned. "I don't want to make the same ones with the second baby." Her toddler was unruly and lacked discipline because Trudy felt weak and had unfulfilled desires of her own. She had been in therapy for several months.

Trudy's friends, family, and caseworker recognized her inability to cope with the first child. They all supported Trudy in her decision to place her second baby for adoption.

Karen

Karen was an adopted child herself. At age seventeen, the most important thing to her was that her child should have two parents. Karen was brought up in a nurturing home and appreciated her father and mother. Over the years, they had often reminded Karen of the excitement in their hearts the day they brought her home.

Karen had a nineteen-year-old friend who was an unmarried mother; she kept her own little boy, Scott. Karen saw Scott as a child who had no one with whom to go fishing or play ball. The strain of trying to be both mom and dad, in Karen's opinion, could be exhausting.

She chose to take the focus off herself and place it on

her child and the child's welfare. She also did not want the stigma of illegitimacy placed on her baby.

As a mature seventeen-year-old, Karen was thoughtful and always doing kind deeds for others, such as volunteer work at the local hospital. She firmly believed the greatest kindness she could give her child was to release him.

Still, her decision didn't come easily. Some of her peers at school gave her a bad time. "People came up to me in the hall and said, 'Oh, how can you do that to your baby, give it away like it's nothing, when babies are just so cute and everything?'

"I told these kids right out that *cute* had nothing to do with it. If they wanted *cute*, they should buy a pet. Babies are not pets. They're people who need all the love in the world."

Karen concluded, "When I'm a parent, I want a husband and a nice place for my family to live."

Terri

"At fourteen, I'm too young, and I recognize that there really isn't any choice in my situation," Terri shared. "My parents say I can't keep the baby, and that's the end of it. Of course, they can't force me to adopt my child out, but I still need a roof over my head.

"What am I supposed to do?" Terri wondered. "Get an apartment? Take my baby to a daycare center on my bike? Lie about my age to get a job—with no work experience?"

The concluding factor for Terri was that her parents would be unhappy if she kept the child, and probably they would make Terri miserable too.

"I couldn't live with that," she said.

After her delivery, Terri will release her baby for adoption. "I dream sometimes about my boyfriend and marrying him. But who is to know if we're going to be right for each other a few years down the road? Besides, I'm only fourteen, way too young to be a wife."

Juliana

"I'm twenty-three and always thought this kind of thing happened to others," said Juliana. "I sure found out otherwise, didn't I?"

Some of her friends who are her age have children and seem content. "It's not that I'm too young to keep this child.

"It's just that I want more than anything to see the baby raised in a two-parent family. I feel everyone deserves a mother and a father. I'm adopted and grateful that my birth mother allowed me to go to a loving home, complete with both parents."

Still, there are times when guilt creeps in. "I guess most anyone my age would feel guilty," she admitted. "But I refuse to let guilt ruin my baby's chances for a decent home life. The way I figure it, I'll make *three* people happy."

It's Not the Easy Way Out

If you choose adoption, be prepared for grief. The separation will be painful. You certainly will hurt emotionally. Placing a child for adoption is almost like a death. You *will* grieve. But your baby won't. This may sound harsh, but there's no need to feel sorry for the baby. Your child will go to a good home and be well provided for. *You* are the one who must deal with this pain and loss, not the baby.

Questions and Answers About Adoption

Q. How long will it take to place my baby in an adoptive home?

A. You should not sign an adoptive consent until after your baby is born. With all the physical and emotional changes that follow delivery, it's important to give yourself time to review the decision to place your child for adoption. Sometimes it takes a few days to grasp the reality of your baby's birth.

Before you leave the hospital, you will sign a *custody release* that allows the baby to be placed in a licensed foster home. You will remain the legally responsible parent until an *adoptive consent* is signed, or until a *termination of parental rights* (TPR) hearing occurs. This usually happens two to eight weeks after the baby's birth.

Q. May I name the baby?

A. Yes. The name you give the baby will go on the original birth certificate, which you will be asked to sign during your stay in the hospital.

The father's last name can be used only with his permission, and it cannot be placed on the birth document without his signature and your permission.

Q. What if I'm not sure, after I have the baby, whether I want to keep the child or place the child for adoption?

A. If you are undecided, it is wise to let the baby continue living in a licensed foster home. This gives you time to think through this important decision without making hasty commitments you may regret later.

These foster homes are caring families that have been screened. They are supervised by the child placement agency. Your baby will be nurtured and loved in a family until the child can go to a permanent home.

You will do both the baby and yourself a favor by taking this time to review and prepare for whatever option you choose. No consent for adoption should be signed until you are *positive* of your decision.

Q. May I see the baby while I'm in the hospital?

A. You maintain your full parental rights while you are there, and you may see the baby as much as you like. In *The Art of Adoption,* Linda Cannon Burgess relates this story:

> People in general and doctors in particular think social workers are cruel in advocating that an unmarried mother see her child before making a decision for adoption. They say, "If she sees the baby, she will never want to give him up." This is the very reason why I encourage mothers to see their babies before making irreversible decisions. If a mother is so uncertain that merely viewing the child would change her mind, she is not ready to relinquish him forever.
>
> I am reminded of a long-distance phone call I received from a mother who had surrendered her baby two years before I joined the agency. She pictured her daughter wasting away in an orphanage. The mother told me that she had married, and the birth of another daughter had renewed thoughts of her first. She was overwhelmed by the conviction that she had abandoned her first child. She was unable to sleep, attend her new baby, or respond to her husband.
>
> I told her that I knew the child had been adopted and promised to find out more. I located the young couple who had adopted the child. In compassion and goodwill for the birth mother, they gave me a detailed account of their daughter's wondrous ways, her appearance, her grace and beauty.
>
> A week later, I was able to relay to the mother all I had been told. She had already come out of her despondency with grateful relief, just to know her

> baby had been adopted. She asked over and over, "What does she look like?" and was pleased by the apparent resemblance to her second child. She struggled to explain: "You see, Mrs. Burgess, I never once laid eyes on my baby. I never saw her. I never held her even once."
>
> Having lived with her baby *in utero* for nine months, having felt her turns and her thrusts, having labored and given birth to her but not to have looked at her—that was, for this sensitive mother, abandonment without love. If with love she had held and blessed her child, she could then have surrendered her for adoption without the burden of future guilt.[2]

It can be good for you to see your child. You can't say good-bye to someone if you've never said hello. However, it's also wise to set limits on how much time you will spend with the baby.

Your maternal instincts may urge you to spend much time with the baby. If you do that, a bond will be growing between you and the baby. You may be setting yourself up for more pain when it is time to let go.

Perhaps you could visit the baby only in the nursery, rather than in your room. Many mothers who have premature infants must visit their babies in the nursery. Therefore, your behavior wouldn't be considered odd if this were your choice.

Another option is to have the baby brought to your room once in the morning and then once again in the evening. Maybe you would prefer only to see the baby immediately following delivery and then for the last time just before your discharge from the hospital.

Some young women choose not to see their babies.

This is a decision you must make for yourself. What may be comfortable for one may not be right for someone else.

On the other hand, some may choose an open adoption plan where identifying information is disclosed. In open adoption, it is wise to complete a written contract to identify the expectations of everyone involved.

It is helpful to know that before or when you arrive at the hospital, you may request *not* to be placed on the maternity floor. Depending on your temperament and your ability to pay the extra cost, you may also ask for a private room if you wish.

If you are still unsure about the importance of seeing the baby, remember that viewing the child will awaken you to the reality of the birth. It can also assist you in starting the grieving process. You need to identify the object of loss. Otherwise, you may remain forever in denial of the birth.

Not seeing the baby would also raise unanswered questions: "Who does he look like? Is she physically all right? What color is his hair?"

Q. If I am a minor, do I need my parents' permission to place my child for adoption?

A. The laws vary from state to state. It is helpful to have your parents' consent, but in many states, it is not required.

Q. Does the baby's father need to consent to the adoption?

A. Every attempt will be made to obtain his consent, because he has a legal right to be involved in the planning for his child, if he is legally recognized as the father. If he is a minor, a consent will also be obtained from his parents, if possible.

If the baby's father is uncooperative and won't sign the

consent, he must at least be served legal notice of the TPR hearing. After he has been notified, he can attend the hearing or waive his rights by not appearing.

Q. What if my child wants to find me when he or she is older?

A. The laws vary from state to state on the disclosure of information from an original birth certificate. In many states, the child may request and obtain this information at the age of nineteen or twenty-one, if the birth parents identified on the birth certificate have authorized disclosure of that information.

Q. Do I have a choice about who adopts my baby?

A. Most agencies will try to locate an adoptive home that matches your reasonable specifications. You will be asked what qualities you're looking for in adoptive parents, such as age, religion, race, hobbies, rural or city residence, and so on.

Almost all agencies are willing to share as much nonidentifying information as you would like to know about the couple. It might help to write out your specific questions about the family. Then when you meet with the social worker or counselor, she can handle your concerns.

Q. How well does the agency know the adoptive parents?

A. The written adoptive application contains details such as the personal history and current situation of the adoptive parents. It includes education, military service, medical history, financial status, employment history, religious affiliation, an autobiography of personal and family history from childhood to the present, and so on.

The adoptive studies generally consist of at least four interviews, statements from three references, verification of and treatment for infertility, verification of their marriage, proof of good health, and clearance by the Bureau of Criminal Apprehension. References will be solicited from their co-workers, pastor, and family physician.

If there is already a school-aged child in the home, a school report is also obtained. The interviews with the adoptive family include in-depth discussions about their marriage, their relationships with children, and their plans for good parenting.

Q. May I have direct contact with the adoptive parents?

A. Agencies now recognize the value of a more open adoption. Earlier, there was no contact between birth and adoptive parents. It was believed that the less the adopted children knew, the better off they were.

With more openness, the agency may arrange for the exchange of pictures and information through the agency for a specified number of years. The sharing of such things helps birth parents work through the grieving and loss. It can assure them that the child is happy and healthy, and thus affirm them in their choice for adoption.

Sometimes the agency might even set up a meeting if all parties are in agreement. The purpose is to give all parties the chance to meet face-to-face. This can be an emotional experience. Usually the meeting affirms the decision and helps the birth parents and adoptive parents feel comfortable with each other.

It's common for birth parents and adoptive parents to want to capture their feelings on paper. Such letters are a sample of the emotions that whirl through hearts, minds, and souls when a baby leaves the birth mother to live with the new family. Here are a few of those heartfelt letters.

Expressions of Love

Dear Adoptive Parents,

When I first became pregnant, I didn't know what to do. I wanted to have an abortion, but soon I realized that I'd be killing a human life. I think that would have been harder to live with. Then I started to think about keeping my baby. But again I soon realized what all it would involve. I'd have to quit high school and my job.

I don't want to sound selfish, but I didn't want to have to give up these things. I wanted to buy a car and go on to more schooling later. So I finally decided to place my baby for adoption.

The decision was not an easy one. I've cried over it many times. But I've learned through all my pain that I have given you a chance of a lifetime. You now have someone who means everything to you. I'm sure that you will love and take care of him as if he were yours through natural birth.

My memories of Josh will always be with me. He is a part of me, and I'm a part of him. But I have to totally let go so that I don't feel like I'm just kidding myself, while I keep hoping I'll see him again.

Someday when I need to share my feelings again, I hope you will accept my letters. I may want to write to Josh, but I'm not sure. He's yours now, and if roles were reversed, I wouldn't want a lot of communication. I would feel like my space was being invaded.

Well, I have to go to class now, so I'll end this. Please take the best care of my little sweetheart. I'll always love him as much as you both do, maybe even more. I wish you the best of luck with Joshua forever.

Love,
Joshua's Birth Mother

• • •

To Angela's New Parents,

Thank you for the wonderful letter you wrote me. It meant a lot since it's the only contact I have had with my daughter. You noted the little things about her that I noticed, too: her brown eyes, beautiful red hair, and her alertness. Enclosed you can find a letter I have written to my little Angela. Please give it to her someday, whether it be ten or twenty-one years from now.

Please never hold back the truth that I love her, because I truly do. Tell Angela I did what I did because I wanted her to have a better life than I have.

Continue to pray for me. I still have a lot of growing to do and need prayers and guidance. My counselor told me you have prayed for me faithfully. I appreciate that!

I have to say good-by now. I am praying for you, your new daughter, and your lives together. I love her, and I love you. I know you will take good care of her and teach Angela all about God and his love.

Sincerely,
Her Birth Mom

• • •

Dear Birth Mother,

How do we express our feelings of gratefulness? We are so thankful for the little "flower" you have so graciously given to us. Roseann is an answer to years of prayer.

Our older son feels special because he knows you wanted him to be Roseann's brother, and he is already becoming the "great protector" of his little sister.

Roseann has a winsome, cheery smile and is responsive to our voices and facial expressions. Friends and relatives have given her many lovely clothes and fun toys. But the most precious gift has come from you. The music box that plays "Brahms Lullaby" represents your love and concern for her.

We can appreciate the difficult decision it must have been for you. Our prayers are with you as you mourn the loss and look on toward your future.

With our heartfelt love,
Roseann's Chosen Family

• • •

Q. What will the adoptive parents know about me?

A. Adoption agencies furnish the prospective parents with a written description of your baby's family history, which you will supply. You will supply background information about yourself that includes medical history; social, educational, and employment background; and facts about family members.

Q. What will the adoptive parents tell my child about me?

A. Agencies encourage adoptive parents to use the word *adoption* occasionally in the child's presence long before the child can possibly understand the meaning of this term. They tell the parents that the adoption should not be kept from the child "until the child is older."

Adoption agencies can recommend specific books to help the child understand about adoption from an early age. One of them, *God Loves My Family,* by Carolyn Owens, is an activity book that parents and child can work on together.[3]

Agencies also point out to adoptive parents that it is important to give the child as much positive information about the child's background as possible. Included will be the assurance that you loved your baby so much that you wanted to be sure the child would have a complete family who would be able to provide a loving home.

Q. Do I need to place my baby through an adoption agency? If I know of a couple who wants to adopt, can I place my baby with them?

A. Some states allow private adoptions. These placements are often arranged by a third party, perhaps an attorney or physician. To be certain that the placement satisfies the laws in your state, check with a licensed adoption agency or your state department of welfare.

There is a clear advantage to working with a licensed agency. The counselors there know you have experienced the normal emotional swings that follow delivery. They would not place you in a position of immediately having to make a final decision on the baby's future.

The child is placed in a licensed foster home, and this gives you time to make your choice. The tentative decision you made before the baby's birth may look entirely different afterward.

There is another advantage to working with an agency. If future counseling or contact is requested, the staff will be available to assist the parties involved in the adoption.

Q. What happens at the hearing for termination of parental rights (TPR)?

A. Each state has its own laws for the TPR hearing. In Minnesota, the hearing is brief, taking about five minutes. Sometimes it is held in the judge's chambers rather than in an official courtroom. You will see a judge but no jury.

Present at the hearing will be you, the father of the baby if he so chooses, your parents or guardian if you are underage, and your social worker or counselor.

You have a right to be represented by an attorney. If you are voluntarily terminating parental rights, your social worker or agency will have the legal documents prepared. If you still want an attorney but can't afford the cost, the county will appoint one. It is your privilege to have the assistance of an attorney, but you don't need one.

The TPR hearing is for *your* benefit. The judge wants to make sure that you are not being pressured, that placing the baby is your own decision, that you have had plenty of time to decide, and that you understand the finality of what you are doing.

The judge will ask you if you realize that you have the first right to parent and if you understand your right to Temporary Assistance for Needy Families (TANF). He'll also want you to tell him in your own words *why* you feel the best interest of the child is served by placing the baby in an adoptive home.

Several days before the hearing, the social worker will give the judge all the legal papers (called affidavits) signed by you. Then at the hearing, the judge will talk with you. When the judge feels confident that you have made a thoughtful and thorough decision, the judge will approve and sign the order for termination of parental rights.

Q. Can I, as a birth mother, locate my child?

A. When you terminate parental rights, you are giving up all rights ever to see the child again. However, if you are interested in a reunion, you may contact the agency that helped you place your child and request assistance.

You may also ask for nonidentifying information about

how the child is doing or ask for direct contact. You must remember, however, that if the child is under nineteen, the adoptive parents can decide whether or not they will provide this information.

If you decide to release your child for adoption, you will want to know about the emotions that follow this decision.

What to Expect Following Delivery

After your baby is born, you may feel excited, content with your decision, and glad the pregnancy is over. However, confusion, panic, and uncertainty may set in. It's perfectly natural and typical to have those ups and downs. You may have deep reservations about saying good-bye. If this happens, review your decision and restudy your options.

You need to know that some friends and relatives won't know how to respond. They may not know what to say. For your own sense of well-being, encourage those friends who can allow you to talk about your baby to come and visit you.

Express your grief openly. Don't let it build inside, only to come out years later. The following interview with one young unwed mother shows that it was good for her to put her thoughts in words.

Trisha Reflects

The day after I found out about my pregnancy, I knew I had to tell my mom. Here's the shocker: For some reason, Mom strongly suspected and wasn't all that surprised! Still, it took her a week before we could talk about the problem.

I tried to look at it from her angle. I knew that if our roles were switched, I'd be mad too. I couldn't tell my dad.

Mom told him. He didn't say a word. It was something he didn't want to discuss.

As soon as Mom knew, she asked me to talk with our pastor. He strongly urged that I find some counseling, and he advised me to take my time in making any decisions.

I have good feelings about the group meetings I attended at the counseling center. The people there helped to show me what other teens in my situation were going through. The group interaction was important to me. It was interesting to listen to the other young women's reactions to their problem and to hear about how their relatives and friends were treating them.

I also made some good friends at the center. I'll never forget when one of the young women said, "It's not fair for me to raise the baby all alone while he [the birth father] is still running around." That statement really hit me!

When I pictured myself placing the baby for adoption, it was tough. I knew I wouldn't be able to see him or know where he lived. I wouldn't have the chance to see his first tooth or be with him for his first haircut.

One thing that helped was that no one pushed me to make my decision. Right from the beginning, I knew there was a lot of time to make that choice. But that worked against me, because I kept putting it off.

The way I finally made my choice for adoption was to think about the pros and cons. If I kept the baby, then I'd need to quit both school and my job, because Mom worked full-time. I wouldn't have money to live elsewhere, and I would likely end up on AFDC. When I wrote the pros and cons on a piece of paper, it was obvious what I should do.

A few people voiced negative reactions. One question

came up most often: "How could you give away your baby?" They tried to make me feel guilty, like I was copping out. But when people asked me, I just explained that I couldn't afford to raise a child, that I'm not the only one responsible for him, and that I felt a one-parent home wouldn't be fair to the baby.

After a while, kids at school said they respected me for my decision. The funny thing, though, was that they didn't come right out and tell me. I had to hear it through the grapevine. I wish they'd have come to me and offered some support.

However, my teachers told me face-to-face that they thought I did the right thing. Of course, my parents were relieved. They wanted me to place the baby for adoption and felt it was best all along.

This experience has matured me. I can make decisions better because now I look at all the angles and then decide. My parents and I have grown closer. We communicate more and talk openly about things now. They support me with love.

I have a few suggestions for any young woman who is going to place her child: Try to get back to work or school as soon as possible. Recognize that people *will* question you about it. They will still wonder, and some may even be critical of you. Don't take their comments too seriously. No one can tell you if it was the right decision or not. You are the only person capable of that.

• • •

If *your* choice, like Trisha's, is to place your child for adoption, what about your feelings?

What Happens Now?

How you cope with loss is up to you. It's wise not to dwell on negatives. Instead, remind yourself of all the positive reasons for this choice.

When you pray, ask God to bless your baby and be with the child and the new family. Most of all, focus your thoughts on the beautiful gift you gave your child—the gift of life and a loving family. Then focus your thoughts on the beautiful gift you gave the adoptive family—a healthy baby.

Of course, it took a "significant other" to help you begin that life. Next you will want to see how your baby's father or your boyfriend fits into the surprise-pregnancy picture.

12

What About Him?

THUS FAR, THIS BOOK HAS focused mainly on you and your baby. Now you will also want to examine what involvement the birth father will have. Is he willing to support you with love, or does he act as if he's never met you before?

It's great if the birth father is your boyfriend and if he is willing to be involved with the pregnancy, because you need a lot of emotional support at this time. However, as Beth is discovering, the reality of the relationship becomes more clear.

Beth is an attractive nineteen-year-old who knows there is no future in her relationship with Todd, aged sixteen. She realizes Todd is not mature enough for an ongoing relationship.

The pregnancy certainly will complicate your relationship. Having a child bonds you together in many ways. This pregnancy will force you to take a serious look at your relationship and make some decisions about what direction you want it to go.

The birth father is important, and he may want to be an active and positive participant in decision making and parenting.

Some pregnancy care centers have groups specifically designed to support birth fathers. If the birth father is willing to go, encourage him to get this kind of counseling early in your pregnancy. If no special groups for birth fathers are available, include him in the counseling you receive. This is important because he will have an impact on the decision regarding this baby.

Sometimes young women just can't predict how their "significant other" will take the idea of suddenly being thrust into the role of a father.

Some Typical Reactions of Birth Fathers

Ryan

Ryan, age twenty-one and unmarried, never expected to be facing this decision of whether to act in the role of a father. He cares deeply for Ann and wants to support her in whatever decision she feels is best.

He is willing to alter his life goals to marry her. Ryan has considered parenting this child himself. He knows it would be a challenge, but he does have a decent job and could postpone college plans.

Brad

At age eighteen, Brad is excited at the prospect of being a father. He is also demanding. His attitude toward Lori is clear: "I have my rights, too, and I will be in that labor room with you."

He has possessive tendencies, yet he is the dependent one in the relationship. Although he has just graduated from high school, he is still quite irresponsible. Nevertheless, he has told Lori that she must keep the baby and marry him.

Tim

Here is a young man who is an expert at avoiding the issue. Since he found out that Patti is pregnant, he has had no contact with her.

Patti, after delivering their child, can't understand why the baby's father doesn't even want to see the baby. The simple reason is that Tim is running scared.

Brian

Brian is cautious. He wants to provide emotional support, but not too much. "I'm afraid I'll be pinned down with the responsibility of a wife and family. If that happens, my goal of becoming an airline pilot will be shot down.

"I guess I prefer for her to give the baby up. If she keeps it, how will I ever pay the child support?"

Johnny

At fifteen, John has a predictably immature reaction. "I don't give a rip what Charla does with the kid. It's not mine anyway. What do I care?"

Johnny really doesn't know how to react, so he puts up defenses. Though he is hurting inside, he appears to be cool and crass.

Tacitus, a historian born around A.D. 56, said, "It is part of human nature to hate the person you have hurt." Johnny's reaction certainly supports this statement. But it's also true that as humans, we tend to hate those who have hurt us.

• • •

You may feel angry because the birth father can go on with his activities without this pregnancy impacting his life in a major way. He may not be taking the responsibility to support you as you think he should.

On the other hand, you might feel guilty because you ended your relationship with him when you discovered you were pregnant. He wanted you to remain his friend and keep the child.

Are you suffering hurt and rejection because you depended on him, and now he has dumped you? This reaction usually brings on the depressing feeling of being used.

On the other hand, you might feel gratitude because he has chosen to stick by you and support you as much as possible, even though you are not ready to marry. With a counselor, the two of you can discuss parenthood and adoption, Together you can make the best decision for your baby.

No matter how the birth father has treated you, he has legal responsibilities to fulfill and legal rights to claim.

What Are His Legal Responsibilities?

Bev O'Brien says it best:

> Our lawyer advised us that if Sandy had a good case against Jim, he would be legally responsible for all the expenses of Sandy's pregnancy, as well as for child support (if Sandy decided to raise her baby herself) until the child reached the age of eighteen. . . .
>
> After assessing the facts, our lawyer felt that Sandy did have a good case, and he recommended sending a letter of demand to Jim. In it, Jim was requested to pay for those expenses Sandy had listed. The letter also notified Jim that he would be subject to payment of further pregnancy-related expenses and possibly child-support payments.

When Jim failed to respond to this action, our lawyer discussed further steps he could take.

"I can either file a claim in court on Sandy's behalf, or I can file a paternity suit against the baby's alleged father. . . ."

He explained what was involved. If necessary, the judge may order medical testing (much improved in reliability in recent years) to establish paternity.

The judge will listen to testimony for both the baby's mother and the alleged father. If, in the judge's opinion, there is reason to believe that the alleged father is indeed the father, then the paternity of the baby is established. In that case, the father is required to pay court costs and whatever expenses and child support the judge decrees.[1]

What Are His Legal Rights?

When paternity has been established, the father has legal responsibilities and legal rights.

If you parent the child, he will be required to provide financial support. Many states are cracking down on this by not allowing loans to be granted or a driver's license to be renewed for someone whose child support payments are not made.

If you are the legally responsible parent, the father might seek visitation rights. That may be beneficial for the child. You might disagree with the father about who should have permanent custody of the child. If that happens, remember that the welfare of the child is most important.

A consultation with an attorney would be valuable. This would help you find answers to specific legal questions.

What's in Store?

No matter what your feelings toward each other, try to look at this time as a period of growth for both of you. This crisis will either draw you closer or drive you apart.

Questions to Consider

1. Would you want the relationship between yourself and your baby's father to be different in any way?
2. How could you improve it?
3. Has your relationship changed recently? How?
4. What kind of relationship would you like the baby to have with the father? What kind of relationship does the father want to have with the baby?
5. If you keep the baby and choose not to marry, what would you want the baby to know about the father? Does the father want to participate in parenting the baby?
6. If the father is your boyfriend, what kind of feelings do you have toward your boyfriend's parents?
7. What interest do you wish the boyfriend's parents to have in the baby?

What About Your Own Parents?

As stated earlier, your pregnancy has also had a profound effect on your parents' lives. For some parents, the shock of an unmarried daughter becoming a mother is bound to erupt in a display of emotional fireworks. The parents may explode at first, then slowly come to accept the situation.

Others may take the news as a not-so-pleasant surprise, but still something they can handle. Your parents may fit into an entirely different category. The next chapter will show how some parents feel about their daughter's unplanned pregnancy.

13

Grandparents Have Feelings, Too

An Open Letter to Parents

DEAR PARENTS,

Dealing with the pressure-cooker emotions that swell with the discovery of an unmarried pregnant daughter, I seesawed from denying it was true, to accepting it, to hoping for a miscarriage, to loving her, to wanting her to go somewhere, have the baby, and pretend it never happened.

On top of everything else, if she chose to complete the pregnancy, this would be our first grandchild. I'm too young to say I had actually dreamed of this day, but the thought had flitted through my mind.

Kind and dear friends told me it happens all the time. *Not to my girl,* I silently screamed. She had played the virgin Mary in a play during high school—and fit the part. How could this happen?

Mary and I went to a pregnancy care center for help. We needed a third person to help us talk and work through our feelings.

We agreed on one thing. We loved each other. This was not going to break up our family. Somehow, whatever our daughter decided, we were going to stick together. Even friends do that.

My suggestion to you as parents is to remain a friend to

your daughter too. No matter what.

Written by one who's been there.

Reactions of Expectant Grandparents

No two people except siblings have the same set of parents. For this reason, if you have a friend who's experienced a crisis pregnancy, your mom and dad probably won't react the way her parents did.

Here are examples of how some parents took the news. You may or may not see your mom and dad among them.

Sarah

Believe it or not, Sarah's parents were pleased when she told them she was pregnant. They both loved babies and were already stand-in grandparents to the neighborhood children. There was no doubt in their minds that they would want to adopt their own flesh and blood.

"We felt we'd been given a second chance at parenting a baby from early infancy, and we anxiously awaited our grandchild's birth," they explained. "Of course, we were unhappy that Sarah chose to loosen the reins on her morals, but we know she's sorry for it, and that's what's important."

Pam

Pam's mom and dad took a different attitude. They wanted her to abort, but she was too far along in the pregnancy. Their next choice was to hide her in a foster home seventy-five miles away.

"I don't know that I can ever forgive her for the shame she's caused us," her mom admitted. "Her dad and I are going for counseling now to try to work through the bitterness."

Tina

Tina's folks absolutely refused to discuss the pregnancy with her. They were trapped in the denial stage. When faced with the actual birth, they felt that Tina had no choice but to place the baby for adoption.

"I'm sorry to have this attitude, but I can't help it," her dad said. "I don't want Tina's kid around to remind me of my failure as a father."

Amy

By contrast, Amy's parents became very close to her through her pregnancy. Amy's mother was pregnant when *she* got married, and she was extremely supportive and sympathetic. She didn't try to influence Amy one way or another. Instead, she allowed her daughter to make her own decisions.

"How could I help but love my daughter through this? We all make mistakes," her mother said. "Not one of us is perfect. What possible good would it do to be angry with her?"

Negative Attitudes Can Change

No matter how your parents first reacted to the crisis pregnancy, their thoughts and feelings may change over the next nine-to-twelve months.

Bev O'Brien shares a touching personal experience in her book *Mom, . . . I'm Pregnant.* After she had a disagreement with her nineteen-year-old pregnant daughter, the daughter left and didn't come home for several hours. She worried about her child's emotional and physical well-being. Then Mrs. O'Brien explains how she stepped onto the road marked "Acceptance."

"During those anxious hours, I discovered the key to my acceptance of Sandy's pregnancy. I had to stop thinking of myself and to begin thinking of Sandy. I had to face that deep chasm that separated my initial reaction from my ultimate acceptance, walk right up to the edge, and make the leap.

"The longer I hesitated, peering down at all those monsters—guilt, fear of the unknown, unwillingness to look truth in the eye, self-pity—the harder it would be to make myself jump."[1]

Many parents, upon first learning of their daughter's pregnancy, will react with anger, hurt, and guilt. Ruth Allen is a mother of six and a pastor's wife. In a poignant passage from *What's the Matter with Christy?* she shares her tender feelings about her youngest daughter's pregnancy:

> Oh, God! There is so much pain inside me.
>
> I am no stranger to trouble—it seems as though I never have been. There's always been physical and mental suffering of some kind for me. But now life is upside down, and it seems as though it will never be right side up.
>
> This is such a bitter disappointment, Lord! Christy's just fifteen; she's just a baby! My precious little girl—pregnant! I don't know what we're going to do.
>
> Right now I can think of so many things we might have done differently. We should never have let her go out on that first date with him. Why didn't we insist? Because we didn't want to fight with her. What a price to pay for keeping the peace!
>
> Why, Lord? Why does my heart ache so? I wonder about me. Is it because of me that some of our children have chosen to walk on paths of rebellion and

pain? That one nightmare follows another?

This pain is too much to bear. I don't know how I can live through another day. Oh, Lord, where are you in the midst of my misery and tears?

But I remember that in the past there were darker days than this one. Through physical and mental illness, through emotional torment, you calmed me and gave me peace and strength that I never knew existed. You have brought me through many stormy seas and troubled waters.

I look to you now, Lord. Help me! Help us![2]

Help for Your Parents

You want your parents to face your pregnancy honestly. No matter what their initial reaction is, realize that it doesn't necessarily change the love they have for you. Be patient! "Time heals all wounds" is a good phrase to remember.

Your mother and father may need counseling to help them deal with their feelings. If they are willing, urge them to meet with your social worker so they too can gain further support.

Put Yourself in Their Shoes

Consider your parents' perception of out-of-wedlock pregnancy. Back when they grew up, it was something criticized. The unwed mother was almost always sent away. She was judged to be *a bad girl* or *a fallen woman.*

Forty years ago, unless there was a hastily arranged wedding, it was almost unheard of to keep the child. Many people still hold standards against premarital sexual relations. Yet now our society is more ready to accept the unwed mother and to deal directly with the situation in a caring way. There are many resources to call on for help.

The Case for Positive Counseling

In previous chapters, we have stressed how important it is for you to seek professional help. It is also wise for your parents to get counseling. There are many excellent reasons why they should talk with an objective professional.

A trained counselor can help to resolve negative feelings like guilt, anger, denial, and frustration. She can also help them to be honest with you in terms of what you can and cannot expect from them.

Most parents are too close to the problem to be objective. Counseling can provide your mother and father with the tools to back off and let you make your own decisions.

A trained professional tries to steer them toward letting go, releasing some control. She will help your parents be alert to your needs. A counselor may help them understand that they are not responsible for your pregnancy or for the choices you make concerning the baby.

It may be hard for your parents to cope with the fact that their daughter is growing up so fast and taking on adult obligations so quickly. If your mom has protected and sheltered you all your life, it's going to be hard for her to suddenly take off on a shopping trip with you to buy maternity clothes. Counseling can help your mom and dad work through the upset, confused feelings they may experience.

Potential for Growing Closer

Your crisis pregnancy may draw your family into a closer relationship. Before their daughter's pregnancy, some parents appear too busy to care. Then an amazing thing happens. In many cases, the family of a pregnant young woman binds together tightly and provides her with emotional support.

Suddenly all their efforts are devoted to uplifting their daughter with positive reinforcement. We hope this holds true for you. We hope you will see your parents' real concern and their desire to offer helpful, loving support.

Some mothers are skillful in talking with their daughters about the changes that occur during pregnancy. This discussion in itself forms a special bonding that wasn't there before. It then becomes more natural for mother and daughter to delve further into sharing their inner thoughts and feelings.

Your months of pregnancy can also be useful as a time of evaluating future goals. Intimacy guidelines may be reestablished. Priorities, when thoroughly discussed with your family, may shed new light on what issues are really important in your life.

A View from the Other Side

In chapter 11 you read about Trisha. Let's see how her mother coped:

> I think going through Trisha's older sister's pregnancy helped me face Trisha's problem. When she got pregnant, I got as much help for her as I could. I knew from past experience that I just had to get professional support for her.
>
> There are lots of benefits gained from counseling. It's been well worth the time and expense involved. I'm so thankful our pastor directed us to a pregnancy care center.
>
> As soon as parents are aware of their daughter's pregnancy, they need to get started with counseling right away.

Whether your parents offer loving support or are totally furious over your condition, one fact remains: God will stand by you and see you through the crisis pregnancy and ever after, too. If you don't already know God, the last chapter can help you get acquainted.

14

Faith Helps

LIKE MOST SINGLE AND PREGNANT young women, you may wonder, *Why, of all people, did this have to happen to me?* Three quotations from *Apples of Gold* may encourage you:

> The diamond cannot be polished without friction, nor can we be perfected without trials.
>
> God never makes us conscious of our weakness except to give us of his strength.
>
> The difference between stumbling blocks and stepping-stones is in the way we use them.[1]

Stumbling Block or Stepping-Stone

Your choice to give another human being a chance at life is in keeping with God's plan. You might believe your pregnancy is a stumbling block, but God wants to turn your experience into a stepping-stone to him.

Psalm 139 applies to *both* your baby and you.

> For it was you who formed my inward parts; you knit me together in my mother's womb. I praise you, for I am fearfully and wonderfully made. Wonderful are your works; that I know very well. My frame was not hidden from you, when I was being made in secret, intricately woven in the depths of the earth. Your eyes

> beheld my unformed substance. In your book were written all the days that were formed for me, when none of them as yet existed. (Psalm 139:13-16)

The Lord saw us before we were born? Mind-boggling, isn't it? God is keenly aware of our situation. The Lord isn't just standing around and watching it happen!

Many times we can't understand why certain things take place in our lives. We call them stumbling blocks. Frightened and cringing in the middle of the tornado, we wonder if God is on vacation. But God needs no rest, even from all our doubts.

Words of faith from Scripture can reassure us: "Even though I walk through the darkest valley, I fear no evil; for you are with me, Lord; your rod and your staff—they comfort me" (Psalm 23:4, adapted).

When Jesus stilled the storm, he was there in the boat with his disciples (Matthew 8:23-27). He promises that he will be with us too: "Remember, I am with you always, to the end of the age" (Matthew 28:20).

From the moment you chose to carry your baby full-term, God chose to bless you because you refused to destroy someone else's life.

However, it's unrealistic to think there won't be any pain, sorrow, or difficulty involved. It's best to look at the situation as a learning experience, a step toward faith, maturity, and emerging as a better person.

Growth Spurts

Here are some excerpts from interviews with pregnant singles who have discovered blessings in seeming brokenness.

Anne

"I never used to be close to my parents until I became pregnant. Then everything changed. For the first time, I felt their love and support for me. But on the other hand, maybe I just opened my eyes and saw them for who they really are—parents who *always* cared. Seeing me in trouble was the key for them to openly express their affection. And for me to receive it."

Shelley

"Before I got pregnant I was only concerned about wearing the latest fashions and getting time off work to go out with my friends. My crisis pregnancy forced me to grow up, make some mature decisions, and figure out what to do with my future."

Rita

"Going through this pregnancy was the most difficult thing I ever did. But I wouldn't have it any other way. I experienced the miracle of life. And through reading the Bible, I also met the Creator of life and his Son, whom I've come to accept and love. As I look back, I *know* it was the love of Jesus that carried me through the last year."

The Lord Will Carry You Too

You are never going to be the same person you were before your pregnancy. God knows those changes can be scary, and he wants you to know he will travel the road right along with you.

You can pray with the psalmist: "I am continually with you; Lord; you hold my right hand. You guide me with your counsel, and afterward you will receive me with honor" (Psalm 73:23-24, adapted).

Even if your parents and family are not supportive, God has ways of helping you. "If my father and mother forsake me, the Lord will take me up" (Psalm 27:10). The Lord will provide caring persons to help you through, and you will sense God's presence.

If you turn to God, he offers you forgiveness for every sin, sexual or otherwise, you have committed. He will help you work things out. God still loves you, no matter what. In Psalm 32:8 the Lord says, "I will instruct you and teach you the way you should go; I will counsel you with my eye upon you."

The Lord will watch over, care for, and love you through the course of your pregnancy and ever afterward. You can believe it. The Lord is a God of truth.

Here is another comforting promise: "Do not fear, for I am with you, do not be afraid, for I am your God; I will strengthen you, I will help you, I will uphold you with my victorious right hand" (Isaiah 41:10). *Uphold* means to support, advocate, and confirm. *God* is your biggest supporter, day and night, year in and year out.

God has the whole world in his hands. Yet he gives special love and gentle care to the "lambs" and the "mother sheep" (Isaiah 40:11).

Grab Hold of God!

Perhaps you would like to be on God's team, but don't know how to make him captain of your life. Believe that God sent his Son Jesus to pay for your sins once and for all on Calvary's cross. Accept forgiveness through Christ.

Read the Bible, God's Word. It's God's love letter to the world, and its wonderful promises are written to *you*. Meet with God's people, who encourage each other in believing God's good news and in living for God.

Becoming a Christian is so simple that many people trip over it. They think that first they must be good people or do nice things to get into heaven. Not true!

The way to take hold of Christ is to confess your sins (*all* of us are sinners), and believe and accept God's perfect gift, which saves you. Then God's Spirit will be changing you from the inside out, so you will want to please God.

Jesus said, "I am the way, and the truth, and the life. No one comes to the Father except through me" (John 14:6). As you believe and learn from Jesus, you assure yourself of a permanent home in heaven.

The problems you face now and the life you live on earth are temporary. God's love is forever. You can, if you choose, rejoice in God's love, which surrounds you throughout your life and beyond. That makes a life worth living!

Suggested Prayer

Dear Lord,

As I make these decisions, please be
before me to show me the right way,
behind me for encouragement,
beside me for friendship,
above me for protection, and
within, to give me your peace.
Amen.

Prayer of Blessing

The pastor, hospital chaplain, or another caring person may adapt this prayer of blessing to use at the hospital with the new mother (or parents) and the newborn baby. The family (or families) and a few close friends may surround them with love and prayers. If so decided, the adoptive parents may also be present.[1]

• • •

Preparation: The prophet Samuel reminds us that children belong to the Lord. Today (*the mother, and the father, as suitable*) is/are giving (*baby's name*) back to God, her/his Creator and Redeemer.

Hannah received her child Samuel as a gift from the Lord. She said, "Therefore I have lent him to the Lord; as long as he lives, he is given to the Lord." Then "she left him there for the Lord," "to minister to the Lord, in the presence of the priest Eli." Hannah was able to make this "gift . . . to the Lord" because she was depending on God as the greatest "Rock" of refuge and strength.

Today we also have "strong confidence" that (*baby's name*) will "have a refuge" and be "blessed by the Lord." May (*baby's name*) also "become a blessing" to the adoptive parents (*names if known*) and many others in his/her lifetime. Let us pray.

• • •

Prayer: Lord, we thank you for the wonderful mystery of (*baby's name*)'s birth. Thank you that she/he arrived safely and in good health. Bless her/him every day with the presence and joy of your gentle Spirit.

We thank you that you have brought new life out of pain and anguish. Thank you for the care and nurture (*mother's name*) gave (*baby's name*) during her/his formative first nine months. She has given (*baby's name*) a wonderful start.

With great difficulty, we say good-bye to (*baby's name*). We can do so because we are confident that you have guided (*mother's name, and father's name, if suitable*) in making this unselfish choice.

Give (*mother's name*) peace and replace her sorrow with joy as she says good-bye to (*baby's name*). Help her to remember that she has (*they have*) made a wise and courageous decision. When (*mother's name*) feels lonely and sad, fill her with your peace that is beyond human understanding.

We give thanks that (*baby's name*) will have parents and (*an older sister/brother, or whoever*) who will love and care for her/him, and teach her/him to respond joyfully to you, her/his Creator. Bless these adoptive parents (*names, if known*). Fill them with patience, wisdom, and unconditional love.

For the privilege of holding (*baby's name*) these few hours, we are profoundly grateful. With trust in your unfailing grace, we release (*baby's name*) to her/his new family and home. Let (*baby's name*) be a blessing in that home and to many other people.

Give us peace for the days to come. Amen.

Statement to the Church Family

A pastor or spiritual counselor may help the new mother's family develop a statement like this. Then in the sharing time of a worship service, the pastor or counselor could read it to the congregation for them.[1]

• • •

Statement: The (*name of family*) has asked me to read this statement to the congregation for them:

We have had an incredible week with a strange combination of intense pain and profound gratitude.

We have experienced—

• the wonderful mystery and joy of birth.

• the joy of holding in our arms a beautiful, healthy baby girl/boy.

• the wonder and bonding of having, for (*one, or* ___) day(s), a (*fourth, or* ___) member in our family.

• the mixture of feelings in meeting the adoptive family, with mother, father, and seven-year-old sister (*adapt to fit*).

• the intense pain of holding our darling baby one last time and saying good-bye.

• the heart-wrenching experience of putting (sending) her/him into the grateful arms of the adoptive mother and father.

• the agony of leaving the hospital with empty arms and breaking hearts.

• the assurance that she/he will be loved and nurtured by her/his new family.

• the trust that God will again fill us with his peace.

We are grateful for the loving support of the (*name of congregation*) church family during this painful and wonderful experience. You have carried us along, and we have received a fresh share of God's forgiveness, grace, healing, and hope.

Through you, we have received the care of the Good Shepherd. Thank you!

—(*Names of family members*)

• • •

Congregational Response: We accept your statement of faith in God through this stressful experience. Our love surrounds you. We pray that the Lord will continue to grant healing and peace to your family.

Notes

Chapter 1: Don't Panic

1. Adapted from Howard J. Clinebell Jr., *Basic Types of Pastoral Counseling,* rev. ed. (Nashville: Abingdon, 1966).

2. Lennart Nilsson, M.D., medical photographer, with text by Lars Hamberger, M.D., *A Child Is Born* (New York: Dell Publishing, 1990), 104.

Chapter 3: What's Happening to Me?

1. March of Dimes Foundation, *Alert Bulletin* 29.

2. Janet R. Johnson and Diane Pankow: *Pre-Natal Care, Loving Before Birth* (Weymouth, Mass.: Life Skills Education, 1989).

3. *FDA Consumer Memo,* Publ. No. 80-1079.

4. Evelyn Zamula, "Drugs and Pregnancy: Often the Two Don't Mix," *FDA Consumer,* June 1989, 9-10.

5. Ibid., 9-10.

Chapter 5: What Are My Options?

1. Sandy Fertman, "Teen Marriages: Happily Never After?" *Teen,* Jan. 1996, 50.

Chapter 7: Am I Ready for Motherhood?

1. Jane Markell and Jane Winn, *Overcoming Stress* (Wheaton, Ill.: Victor Books, 1982), 90-91.

2. Chart from Ibid., 90-91.

Chapter 8: Money Matters

1. Vanessa O'Connell, "Budgeting for Baby," *Working Woman,* Apr. 1997, 14.

Chapter 11: Making Plans for Adoption

1. This account by "Holly" is used with her permission. All names have been changed.

2. Linda Cannon Burgess, *The Art of Adoption* (New York: © copyright W. W. Norton, 1981), 25. Used by permission.

3. Carolyn Owens, *God Loves My Family* (St. Louis: Concordia Publishing, 1995).

Chapter 12: What About Him?

1. Bev O'Brien, *Mom, . . . I'm Pregnant* (Wheaton, Ill.: Tyndale House, 1982), 85-87, slightly adapted.

Chapter 13: Grandparents Have Feelings, Too

1. Bev O'Brien, "*Mom, . . . I'm Pregnant*" (Wheaton, Ill.: Tyndale House, 1982), 19.

2. Ruth Allen, "*What's the Matter with Christy?*" (Minneapolis: © copyright Bethany House, 1982), 15-16. Used by permission.

Chapter 14: Faith Helps

1. Jo Petty, compiler, *Apples of Gold* (Norwalk, Conn.: C. R. Gibson, 1962), 44, 46, adapted.

Prayer of Blessing

1. Used by permission, from *LifeLines*, published by Bethany Christian Service, 901 Eastern Ave. NE, Grand Rapids, MI 49503-1295. Originally composed by the father of an unwed mother. Adapted and further developed. Scripture references: 1 Samuel 1–2; 1:28; 2:11; 2:20; 2:1-2; Proverbs 14:26; Isaiah 65:23; Psalm 37:26.

Statement to the Church Family

1. Used by permission, from an unmarried mother's family. Adapted and further developed.

Bibliography

Allen, Ruth. *"What's the Matter with Christy?"* Minneapolis: Bethany House, 1982.

Burgess, Linda Cannon. *The Art of Adoption*. New York: W. W. Norton, 1981.

Clinebell, Howard J., Jr. *Basic Types of Pastoral Counseling*. Rev. ed. Nashville: Abingdon, 1966.

FDA Consumer. June 1989, 9-10.

Fertman, Sandy. "Teen Marriages: Happily Never After?" *Teen*, Jan. 1996, 50.

"Health Tips." A publication of the California Medical and Research Foundation. Index WH-45. March 1989.

Johnson, R. Janet, and Diane Pankow. *Prenatal Care: Loving Before Birth*. Weymouth, Mass.: Life Skills Education, 1989.

March of Dimes Foundation Alert Bulletin 29. White Plains, N.Y.: National Foundation Headquarters.

Markell, Jane, and Jane Winn. *Overcoming Stress*. Wheaton, Ill.: Victor Books, 1982.

Morrison, Margaret. "When Your Baby's Life Is So Much Your Own." *FDA Consumer* 13 (May 1979).

Nilsson, Lennart, M.D., medical photographer, with text by Lars Hamberger, M.D. *A Child Is Born*. New York: Dell Publishing, 1990.

O'Brien, Bev. "Mom, . . . I'm Pregnant." Wheaton, Ill.: Tyndale House, 1982.

O'Connell, Vanessa. "Budgeting for Baby." *Working Mother*, Apr. 1997, 14.

Owens, Carolyn. *God Loves My Family*. St. Louis: Concordia Publishing, 1995.

Petty, Jo, compiler. *Apples of Gold*. Norwalk, Conn.: C. R. Gibson Co., 1962.

Reading Suggestions

Allen, Ruth. "*What's the Matter with Christy?*" Minneapolis: Bethany House, 1982.

Ashley, Meg. *Meg: A True Story.* Wheaton, Ill.: Tyndale House, Living Books, 1980.

Dobson, James. *Parenting Isn't for Cowards.* Waco, Tex.: Word Books, 1988.

Johnson, Lisa Halls. *Just Like Ice Cream.* Wheaton, Ill.: Tyndale House, 1995.

Lindsay, Jeanne Warren. *Pregnant? Adoption Is an Option.* Buena Park, Calif.: Morning Glory, 1997.

Lush, Jean, and Pam Vredevelt. *Women and Stress.* Grand Rapids: Fleming H. Revell, Baker Book House, 1992.

O'Brien, Bev. "*Mom, . . . I'm Pregnant.*" Wheaton, Ill.: Tyndale House Publishers, 1982.

Shaffer, Betty. *Lisa.* Minneapolis: Bethany House, 1982.

Zimmerman, Martha. *Should I Keep My Baby?* Minneapolis: Bethany House, 1997.

Pregnancy Care Centers

These centers in Canada and USA appear alphabetically by provinces, states, and cities. The phone number is a *help line* or, failing that, a business line. This list of centers is printed with permission of Care Net, a ministry of CACEMF, August 1998 (703-478-5661). Care Net has a toll-free number for USA and offers to connect callers to a near-by care center: 1-800-395-HELP. # = Suite. Bx = Box.

CANADA

ALBERTA

Calgary PCC
602 11th St. SW, # 408
Calgary, AB T2R 3K6
403-269-3110

Preg. Couns. Ctr.
10089 Jasper Ave., # 700
Edmonton, AB T5J 1V1
403-424-2525

Central Alberta PCC
Lower Main, 4820 Gaetz Ave.
Red Deer, AB T4N 4A4
403-343-1611

BRITISH COLUMBIA

CPC, Surrey
7337 137th St., # 306
Surrey, BC V3W 1A4
604-596-3611

CPC, Vancouver
1675 W. 8th Ave., # 320
Vancouver, BC V6J 1V2
604-731-1122

NEW BRUNSWICK

Greater Moncton CPC
27 John, PO Bx 1208
Moncton, NB E1C 8P9
506-857-3033

Fundy CPC
115 Hazen
St. John, NB E2L 3L3
506-634-8672

ONTARIO

Life Centre
141 Kennedy Rd. N.
Brampton, ON L6V 1X9
905-454-2191

Peterborough CPC
326A Charlotte
Peterborough, ON K9J 2V7
705-742-4015

Lambton CPC
551 Exmouth
Sarnia, ON N7T 5P6
519-383-7115

UNITED STATES (USA)

ALASKA

Anchorage CPC
2902 Boniface Pkwy.
Anchorage, AK 99517
907-337-9292

Eagle River CPC
12801 Old Glenn Hwy.
Eagle River, AK 99577
907-694-1747

CPC, Fairbanks
3678 Thomas, PO Bx 82522
Fairbanks, AK 99708
907-455-8255

Preg. Res. Ctr., North Pole
145 Santa Claus Ln.
PO Bx 82522
Fairbanks, AK 99708
907-488-8111

Homer CPC
3896 Bartlett, PO Bx 2
Homer, AK 99603
907-235-7899

CPC, Juneau
9328 Glacier Hwy.
PO Bx 32204
Juneau, AK 99803
907-789-9599

ABC CPC
508 S. Willow, # D
Kenai, AK 99611
907-283-9062

Valley CPC
2650 Broadview Ave., # 102
Wasilla, AK 99654
907-373-3456

ARIZONA

Pregnancy Care
2176 McCulloch Blvd., # 2
Lake Havasu City, AZ 86403
520-855-2273

Life CPC
723 E. Gurley
Prescott, AZ 86301-3240
520-778-7654

We Care CPS
1879 Peppertree Dr., # A-19
PO Bx 1546
Safford, AZ 85548
520-428-9406

We Care CPS
222 E. Fry Blvd, # E
Sierra Vista, AZ 85635
520-459-5683

CPCs of Tucson (adm.)
2502 N. Alvernon Way
Tucson, AZ 85712
520-321-9765

Women's Preg. Ctr., Central
1124 N. 3rd St.
Tucson, AZ 85705
520-622-5774

Women's Preg. Ctr., Eastside
5714 E. 22nd St.
Tucson, AZ 85711
520-622-5774

ARKANSAS

Life Choices
PO Bx 1345
224 Halter Bldg., PO Bx 1345
Conway, AR 72033
800-395-4357

Central AR CPC
2212 Main
N. Little Rock, AR 72114
501-223-9846

CALIFORNIA

Preg. Ctrs., Contra Costa
2 Park Ln.
Antioch, CA 94509
510-706-0100

Tree of Life Preg. Support Ctr.
5810 Traffic Way
Atascadero, CA 93422
805-461-3405

Bakersfield CPC
2920 F St., # C-5
Bakersfield, CA 93301-1829
805-326-1907

Silent Voices
355 K St., # H
Chula Vista, CA 91911-1209
619-422-0757

Preg. Ctrs., Contra Costa
4991 Clayton Rd.
Concord, CA 94521
925-827-0100

PCC, Crescent City
484 J St., PO Bx 861
Crescent City, CA 95531
707-464-3233

Davis CPC
328 D St., PO Bx 283
Davis, CA 95616
530-753-5433

Living Help Ctr.
10642 Downey Ave., # 107
Downey, CA 90241
562-923-4357

Valley CPC
7660 Amador Valley Blvd., # D
Dublin, CA 94568
925-828-4458

PCC
237 Avocado Ave., PO Bx 1037
El Cajon, CA 92022
219-442-4357

Alternatives Preg. Care Clinic
257 E. 2nd Ave.
Escondido, CA 92025
760-741-9796

Central Valley CPC
3030 N. Fresno, # 200
Fresno, CA 93703-1124
559-225-8854

Preg. Help Clinic, Glendale
1911 W. Glenoaks Blvd., # A
Glendale, CA 91201
818-843-0424

Kings Co. CPC
206 W. Lacey Blvd., # A
PO Bx 135
Hanford, CA 93232
209-583-1900

Preg. Help Clinic, Hollywood
1131 N. Vermont Ave, # 107
Hollywood, CA 90029
213-913-1975

Antelope Pregnancy Coun. Ctr.
44739 N Date
Lancaster, CA 93539
805-942-0829

CPC, Lodi
1110 W. Kettleman Ln., # 34
Lodi, CA 95240
209-368-7190

Preg. Support Ctr., Lompoc
104 S. C St., PO Bx 2353
Lompoc, CA 93438
805-735-2353

PCCs of San Mateo Co.
728 B Willow Rd.
Menlo Park, CA 94025
800-395-4357

Alpha CPC
645 W. Olive Ave, # 321
Merced, CA 95348-2433
209-383-4700

Modesto Preg. Ctr.
3025 McHenry Ave., # M
Modesto, CA 95350
209-526-1734

South Valley PCC
84 W. 2nd St.
Morgan Hill, CA 95037
408-778-1175

Santa Clarita Valley PC
24359 Walnut
Newhall, CA 91321
805-255-0082

CPC, San Fernando Valley
16909 Parthenia, # 301
North Hills, CA 91343
818-830-1200

Helping Hands Preg. &
Parenting Ctr.
PO Bx 3261
Oakhurst, CA 93644
209-642-2229

Dayspring CPC
815 Elliott Rd.
Paradise, CA 95969
916-876-1113

Ramona PCC
1530 Main St., # 6
Ramona, CA 92065
760-789-7059

CPC, Salinas
75 San Miguel Ave., # 6
PO Bx 4915
Salinas, CA 93912-4915
408-757-5500

PCCs of San Mateo Co.
1650 Laurel
San Carlos, CA 94070
800-395-4357

CPC, San Francisco
1350 A Lawton
San Francisco, CA 94122
415-753-8000

Birth Choice, San Marcos
277 S. Rancho Sante Fe Rd., # S
San Marcos, CA 92069
760-744-1313

Life Network
123 W. Padre, # 3, PO Bx 3668
Santa Barbara, CA 93101
805-569-3050

Central Coast Preg. Ctr.
500 S. Broadway, # 110A
PO Bx 6996
Santa Maria, CA 93456-6996
805-928-9285

Preg. Couns. Ctr., Sonoma Co.
750 Mendocino Ave., # 1
Santa Rosa, CA 95401-4822
707-575-9000

CPC, Simi Valley
2955 Cochran, # 202B
Simi Valley, CA 93065
805-583-3590

CPC, Tehachapi
430 W. J St.
Tehachapi, CA 93581
805-823-8255

CPC, Tracy
1680 Hurley Ct., PO Bx 1237
Tracy, CA 95378-1237
209-836-4415

Preg. Couns. Ctr., Ukiah
331 N. School
Ukiah, CA 95482-4311
707-463-1436

COLORADO

CO Preg. Ctrs.
2295 S. Chambers Rd., # I
Aurora, CO 80014-4544
303-695-4600

Boulder Caring Preg. Ctr.
350 Broadway, # 40
Boulder, CO 80303-3340
303-494-3262

Campus Caring Preg. Ctr.
U. of CO
UMC 337, Campus Bx 207
Boulder, CO 80309
303-492-8778

CO Preg. Ctrs.-Eastern Plains
211 S. Owens, PO Bx 41
Byers, CO 80103
303-822-9368

Montezuma CPC,
Heart to Heart
23 S. Market, PO Bx 716
Cortez, CO 81321
970-565-0979

The Preg. Ctr.
1315 Main Ave., # 230
Durango, CO 81301
970-247-5559

Estes Valley Caring Preg. Ctr.
Lwr. Stanley Village
PO Bx 1503
Estes Park, CO 80517
970-586-2422

Mountain Area Preg. Ctr.
6949 Hwy. 73
Evergreen, CO 80439
303-674-5881

Valley CPC
PO Bx 837
Glenwood Springs, CO 81602
970-945-5562

CPC, N. Colorado
821 9th St., # 1
Greeley, CO 80631-1133
970-353-2673

Arkansas Valley Preg. Ctr.
211 Belleview Ave.
LaJunta, CO 81050
719-384-5561

Life Choices Preg. Ctr.
20 Mountain View Ave.
Longmont, CO 80501
303-651-2050

CPC, Montrose
231 S. 4th St., PO Bx 563
Montrose, CO 81402
970-249-4302

Caring Preg. Ctr., Pueblo
500 Colorado Ave.
Pueblo, CO 81004
719-544-9312

CONNECTICUT

Hope For Life
126 Main
Cheshire, CT 06410
203-271-2703

Caring Families Preg. Svcs.
16 J Maple
Danielson, CT 06239
860-779-0218

Preg. Support Ctr.
340 Long Hill Rd., PO Bx 211
Groton, CT 06340
860-448-2990

A Better Choice Women's Ctr.
120 Wash., # 27, PO Bx 1364
Middletown, CT 06249
860-344-9292

Hopeline Women's Ctr.
500 Monroe Tpk.
Monroe, CT 06468
203-261-4673

Unionville CPC
30 Mill
Unionville, CT 06085
860-673-7397

DELAWARE

Door of Hope (main ofc.)
2884 Summit Bridge Rd.
Bear, DE 19701
302-834-4696

Sussex Co. Preg. Ctr.
536 S. Bedford St. Ext.
Georgetown, DE 19947-1852
302-856-4344

Door of Hope, Newark
16 Tyre Ave.
Newark, DE 19711
302-834-4696

Door of Hope, Wilmington
2414 Penna. Ave.
Wilmington, DE 19806
302-834-4696

DISTRICT OF COLUMBIA

Capitol Hill CPC
713 Maryland Ave. NE
Washington, DC 20002
202-546-1019

FLORIDA

First Care Preg. Ctrs.
644 Glades Rd.
Boca Raton, FL 33431
561-392-3446

Manasota Care Net CPC
5550 26th St. W., # 1
Bradenton, FL 34209
941-751-1966

First Care Preg. Ctrs.
6275 W. Sample Rd.
Coral Springs, FL 33067
954-752-7747

Hope Preg. Ctrs., Broward
3700 SW 64th Ave.
PO Bx 290061
Davie, FL 33329-0061
954-581-6991

Hope Preg. Ctrs.
823 E. Oakland Park Blvd.
Ft. Lauderdale, FL 33334
954-568-2616

Woman's Preg. Ctr.
257 N. Krome Ave.
Homestead, FL 33030
305-245-4673

First Coast Women's Svcs.
3938 Sunbeam Rd., # 3
Jacksonville, FL 32257
904-262-6300

First Care Preg. Ctrs.
711 W. Indiantown Rd., # A-4
Jupiter, FL 33458
561-744-2644

First Care Preg. Ctrs.
1123 Crestwood Ave.
Lake Worth, FL 33460
561-547-8790

Preg. Resources
2225 S. Babcock
Melbourne, FL 32901
407-724-6202

Woman's Preg. Ctr.
5975 Sunset Dr., # 101
Miami, FL 33143
305-665-4673

Hope Preg. Ctrs., Broward Co.
9927 Miramar Pkwy.
Miramar, FL 33025
954-442-9638

True Life Choice
4314 Edgewater Dr.
Orlando, FL 32804-2135
407-294-4314

Preg. Ctr., Pinellas Co.
9745 66th St. N.
Pinellas Park, FL 33782
813-545-1234

Crisis Pregnancy Services
8432 S. Federal Hwy.
Port St. Lucie, FL 34952
800-395-4357

Preg. Ctr., Pinellas Co.
4326 Central Ave.
St. Petersburg, FL 33711
813-328 0228

Women's Preg. Ctr.
1225 Miccosukee Rd.
Tallahassee, FL 32308-5007
850-877-4774

Woman's Place Ministries
4311 W. Waters Ave., # 302
Tampa, FL 33614-1980
800-267-7900

PCC, Temple Terrace
7628 N. 56th St., # 14
Tampa, FL 33617
813-978-9737

University Area Preg. Ctr.
12310 N. Nebraska Ave.
Tampa, FL 33612-5336
813-978-9737

Vero Beach CPC
1503 24th St., PO Bx 836
Vero Beach, FL 32961
561-569-7939

First Care Preg. Ctrs.
2215 N. Military Tr., # A-4
W. Palm Beach, FL 33409-2901
561-478-2644

GEORGIA

Augusta Care Preg. Ctr.
1298½ Broad, PO Bx 1775
Augusta, GA 30903
706-724-3733

CPC, Coastal GA
3365 Cypress Mill Rd., # 7
Brunswick, GA 31520
912-267-1100

PCC, Douglas Co.
3697 Kings Hwy.
Douglasville, GA 30135
770-920-1000

Gilmer Preg. Ctr.
135 Village Way, PO Bx 383
Ellijay, GA 30540
706-276-1945

PCC, Perry
1104 Meeting, PO Bx 382
Perry, GA 31069
912-988-8199

The HOPE Ctr.
9740 Main, # 120, PO Bx 384
Woodstock, GA 30188
770-924-0864

IDAHO

Wood River Preg. Ctr.
17 E. Bullion, PO Bx 441
Hailey, ID 83333
208-788-2429

Preg. Care Ctr.
1448 G St.
Lewistown, ID 83501
208-746-9704

Open Door Preg. Ctr.
312 S. Washington
Moscow, ID 83843
208-882-2370

Lifeline PCC
1323 12th Ave. S.
Nampa, ID 83651
208-466-4000

PCCare Ctr., Sandpoint
311 N. 2nd St., PO Bx 1107
Sandpoint, ID 83864
208-263-7621

ILLINOIS

Preg. Info. Ctr.
205 N. Lake
Aurora, IL 60506
630-896-8600

CPC, Eastern IL
914 Monroe Ave.
Charleston, IL 61920
217-345-5000

PASS, PCCs
2219 S. Exchange
Crete, IL 60417
708-672-0841

Tri-County CPC
416 Virginia, # 2
Crystal Lake, IL 60014
815-455-0965

New Life Preg. Ctr.
240 W. Main
Decatur, IL 62523
217-429-0464

We Care Preg. Ctr.
1260 Oakwood Ave.
DeKalb, IL 60115
815-748-4242

Hope CPC
404 N. Galena Ave.
Dixon, IL 61021
815-625-5300

Family Life PCC
604 N. Linden, PO Bx 154
Effingham, IL 62401
800-600-2966

Freeport Preg. Ctr.
224 W. Stephenson
Freeport, IL 61032
815-232-5433

Arms of Love CPC
4854 N. Alby, PO Bx 157
Godfrey, IL 62035
618-466-1690

CPC, Eastern IL
2520 Marshall
Mattoon, IL 61938
217-234-3312

CPC, Greater Quad Cities
829 15th St.
Moline, IL 61265
309-797-3636

Caring Preg Ctr.
202 N. Main, PO Bx 417
Pontiac, IL 61764
815-842-2484

Quincy CPC
311 N. 5th St., # 103, PO Bx 441
Quincy, IL 62306
217-223-8200

Rockford Area PPC
2501 Broadway
Rockford, IL 61108-5752
815-398-5444

Friend in Need PCC
225 W. Wash., PO Bx 137
Rushville, IL 62681
800-424-1991

South Central PCC
209 S. Walnut
Salem, IL 62881
618-548-3111

PASS, PCCs
613 E. 162nd St.
South Holland, IL 60473
708-331-7733

Hope CPC
2323 E. Lincolnway
Sterling, IL 61081
815-625-5300

PASS, PCCs
17214 S. Oak Park Ave.
Tinley Park, IL 60477
708-614-9777

New Beginnings Women's Ctr.
208 E. Walnut, # 104
Watseka, IL 60970-0013
815-432-6778

Tri-County CPC
459 W. Liberty
Wauconda, IL 60084
847-526-0960

CPS, DuPage Co.
671 N. Cass Ave.
Westmont, IL 60559
630-455-0300

INDIANA

Alpha PCC
24 W. 17th St.
Anderson, IN 46016
765-649-0449

CPC, Bloomington
223 Pete Ellis Dr., # 28
PO Bx 5926
Bloomington, IN 47407-5926
812-334-0055

Brazil CPC
20 N. Meridian
Brazil, IN 47834
812-448-3444

PCC, Columbus
801 3rd St., PO Bx 2215
Columbus, IN 47202-2215
812-378-4114

CPC, Indianapolis-Avon
47 N. CR 625 E.
Danville, IN 46122
317-272-3056

Fort Wayne CPC
3030 Lake Ave., # 20
Fort Wayne, IN 46805-5428
219-422-3544

CPC, Putnam Co.
1211 S. Bloomington
Greencastle, IN 46135
765-653-3345

Central Indiana CPC
2413 N. Meridian, # 201
Indianapolis, IN 46208
317-925-5437

CPC, Indianapolis-East
1007 N. Arlington Ave.
Indianapolis, IN 46219
317-359-1600

CPC, Indianapolis-North
7350 N. Keystone
Indianapolis, IN 46240
317-259-1222

CPC, Indianapolis-South
528 N. Turtle Creek Dr, # 4
Indianapolis, IN 46227
317-783-1601

CPC, Indianapolis-West
2732 Lafayette Rd.
Indianapolis, IN 46222
317-923-9030

Boone Co. CPC
115 N. West St.
Lebanon, IN 46052
765-482-3306

PCC, Morgan Co.
609 Morton Ave.
Martinsville, IN 46151
765-342-7256

Lake Co. Women's Ctr.
64 W. 80th Place, PO Bx 10066
Merrillville, IN 46410
219-769-4321

PASS, PCCs
Environ Plaza, 514 E. 86th Ave.
Merrillville, IN 46410
219-769-3112

Heart to Heart PCC
600 S. Tillotson Ave.
Muncie, IN 47304
765-286-6060

Henry Co. PCC
540 S. Main, # 2
New Castle, IN 47362
765-529-7298

L.I.F.E. Preg. Help Ctr.
650 N. Gospel, # 2
Paoli, IN 47454
812-723-3689

PCC, Jay Co.
1754 W. 100 South
Portland, IN 47371
219-726-8636

New Beginnings CPC
219 N. Fletcher, PO Bx 313
Spencer, IN 47460
812-829-2229

CPC, Wabash Valley
1527 Poplar, PO Bx 3447
Terre Haute, IN 47803-0447
812-234-8059

CPC, Johnson Co.
180 N. US 31
Whiteland, IN 46184
317-535-6396

PCC, Randolph Co.
301 W. North St.
Winchester. IN 47394-1518
800-705-5571

IOWA

CPC, Greater Quad Cities
2706 W. Central Park
Davenport, IA 52803
319-386-3737

Caring Preg. Ctr.
1631 4th St. SW, # 124
Mason City, IA 50401
515-424-2237

Preg. Ctr., Central IA
709 First Ave. W., PO Bx 694
Newton, IA 50208
515-792-3050

Heartland Preg. Ctr.
101 S. Market, # 302
Ottumwa, IA 52501
515-683-3030

PCC, Pella
808½ Wash., PO Bx 282
Pella, IA 50219
515-628-4827

KANSAS

Midwest PCC
213 E. Main, PO Bx 981
Independence, KS 67301-0981
316-331-2812

Heartland PCC
1027D Wash. Rd., PO Bx 762
Newton, KS 67114
800-536-7338
945-9400

KENTUCKY

Haven of Hope
103 W. 11th St., PO Bx 645
Benton, KY 42025
800-395-1761

Preg. Support Ctr.
1439 Magnolia, PO Bx 9953
Bowling Green, KY 42102-9953
502-781-5050

Marsha's Place PCC
603 Center
Henderson, KY 42420
502-826-9674

Door of Hope PCC
95 YMCA Dr., PO Bx 371
Madisonville, KY 42431
502-821-9825

Hope for Life PCC
319 S. 9th St., PO Bx 5353
Mayfield, KY 42066
502-247-3190

Shelter of Love CPC
107 W. Main, PO Bx 393
Morganfield, KY 42437
502-389-2847

Life House Care Ctr.
1506 Chestnut
Murray, KY 42071
502-753-0700

Hope Unlimited PCC
2330 Cairo Rd., PO Bx 7403
Paducah, KY 42001-7403
502-442-1166

LOUISIANA

Ark-La-Tex CPC, Bossier Ctr.
2284 Benton Rd, # D-201
Bossier City, LA 71101
318-741-0101

Northlake CPC
814 W. 21st St., PO Bx 3198
Covington, LA 70434
504-893-4281

Ark-La-Tex CPC
4449 Youree Dr., PO Bx 5087
Shreveport, LA 71135-5087
800-939-9997

MAINE

PCC, Aroostook Co.
28 Houlton Rd., PO Bx 1553
Presque Isle, ME 04769
207-764-0022

Abri CPC
389B Main
Rockland, ME 04841
800-835-1611

MARYLAND

Bowie Crofton Preg. Ctr.
4375 Northview Dr.
Bowie, MD 20716
301-262-1330

Frederick Co. CPC
45 Waverley Dr.
Frederick, MD 21702
301-662-5300

Laurel Preg. Ctr.
415 Main, # 4
Laurel, MD 20707
301-776-9996

PCC, Southern MD
22335 Exploration Dr., # 2020
PO Bx 31
Lexington Park, MD 20653
800-395-4357

Alpha PCC
218 Main
Reisterstown, MD 21136
410-833-7793

Rockville Preg. Ctr.
12022 Parklawn Dr.
Rockville, MD 20852
800-492-5530

Catherine Foundation PCC
3065 Old Wash. Rd.
Waldorf, MD 20601
800-492-5530

MASSACHUSETTS

Daybreak PCC
3 Park, 3rd Floor
Boston, MA 02108
617-742-9171

PCC, Merrimack Valley
496 Main
Haverhill, MA 01830
978-373-5700

Springfield CPC
708 Sumner Ave.
Springfield, MA 01138
413-732-2006

MICHIGAN

CPC Preg. Couns. & Svcs.
153 N. Main, PO Bx 928
Adrian, MI 49221
517-263-5701

Crisis Preg. Info. Ctr.
28913 Woodward Ave.
Berkley, MI 48072-0923
248-545-6508

Positive Alternatives
194 N. State, # 205
Caro, MI 48723
517-672-4673

Bethany LifeLine
901 Eastern Ave. NE, PO Bx 294
Grand Rapids, MI 49501-0294
800-238-4269

Lakeshore Preg. Ctr.
90 W. 8th St.
Holland, MI 49423
616-396-5840

Lapeer Preg., Family Care Ctr.
2188 W. Genesee, # 2
Lapeer, MI 48446
810-667-0055

CPS, Midland
2828 N. Saginaw
Midland, MI 48640-2634
517-835-1500

Central MI Preg. Svcs.
623 E. Broadway, PO Bx 806
Mt. Pleasant, MI 48804-0806
517-773-6008

Compassion PC, Macomb Co.
30464 23 Mile Rd.
New Baltimore, MI 48047
810-949-2229

Niles PCC
1011 Broadway
Niles, MI 49120
616-684-6200

CPC, Char-Em
231 State
Petoskey, MI 49770
800-238-4269

Chippewa Co. CPC
409 Ashmun, # 200
Sault Ste. Marie, MI 49783
906-635-1103

Preg. Resource Ctr., T. C.
1040 Walnut, PO Bx 5363
Traverse City, MI 49696
616-946-0911

MINNESOTA

Lakes Area Preg. Support Ctr.
416 Charles
Brainerd, MN 56401
218-825-0793

Amnion CPC
13775 Nicollet Ave. S.
Burnsville, MN 55337
612-898-4357

Cambridge CPC
117 S. Ashland, PO Bx 61
Cambridge, MN 55008
612-689-4319

Caring Preg. Ctr.
121 N. Main, PO Bx 51
Fairmont, MN 56031-0051
507-238-2255

Rum River CPC
155 2nd Ave. SW, # 2
Milaca, MN 56353
320-983-3771

Mora CPC
600 S. Union
Mora, MN 55051
320-679-4493

Caring PC, Park Rapids
601 E. First St., PO Bx 754
Park Rapids, MN 56470
218-732-5212

Rum River CPC
501 S. 4th St.
Princeton, MN 55371
612-389-0950

St. Cloud CPC
400 E. St. Germain
St. Cloud, MN 56304
320-253-1962

Helping Hand Preg. Ctr.
919 4th Ave.
Worthington, MN 56187-2326
800-395-4357

MISSISSIPPI

Golden Triangle CPC
1909½ Hwy. 45 N, PO Bx 9334
Columbus, MS 39705-9334
601-327-0500

Golden Triangle CPC
102 Old West Point Rd.
Starkville, MS 39759
601-323-1700

MISSOURI

Kirksville CPC
902 E. LaHarpe, # 116
PO Bx 663
Kirksville, MO 63501
816-665-5688

Precious Life PCC
10640 Baptist Church Rd.
St. Louis, MO 63128
314-843-8767

Precious Life PCC-Cedar Hill
8255 Local Hillsboro Rd.
Cedar Hill, MO 63016
314-285-4116

MONTANA

Billings CPC
2323 Broadwater Ave,
PO Bx 80146
Billings, MT 59102
406-652-4868

NEBRASKA

Lincoln CPC
745 S. 9th St.
Lincoln, NE 68508-3107
402-475-2501

Birthline Ctr.
111 E. C St., PO Bx 1893
North Platte, NE 69103
308-534-3085

AAA CPC
9006 Ohio
Omaha, NE 68134
402-397-0600

NEVADA

CPC, Las Vegas
721 E. Charleston Blvd, # 6
Las Vegas, NV 89104
702-366-0764

CPC, Pahrump
1471 E. Hwy. 372, PO Bx 4620
Pahrump, NV 89041
702-751-2229

Reno-Sparks CPC
200 Brinkby Ave.
Reno, NV 89509
702-826-1999

NEW HAMPSHIRE

Concord PCC
7 Greenwood Ave.
Concord, NH 03301
603-224-7477

Sure Hope CPC
14 W. Main, PO Bx 771
Hillsboro, NH 03244-0771
603-464-3299

Preg. Res. Ctr., Monadnock
28 Court St.
Keene, NH 03431
603-358-6460

Lakes Region PCC
506 Union Ave, # 2
Laconia, NH 03246
603-528-3121

CPC, Manchester
50 Bridge
Manchester, NH 03101
603-623-1122

CPC, Nashua
12 Front
Nashua, NH 03060
603-883-1122

Dayspring PCC
52 Main, # 4-5
Newport, NH 03773
603-863-3996

Preg. Res. Ctr., Monadnock
23 Elm
Peterborough. NH 03458
603-924-8788

PCC, White Mountains
35 Main, PO Bx 923
Plymouth, NH 03264
603-536-2111

Dayspring PCC
1 Main, # 2
West Lebanon, NH 03784
800-344-4272

NEW JERSEY

Friendship PC, Hunterdon Co.
168 Main
Flemington, NJ 08822
908-806-4444

Friendship Preg. Ctrs.
297 Griffith
Jersey City, NJ 07307
973-538-0967

Alpha Preg. Ctr.
1764 Brunswick Ave.
Lawrenceville, NJ 08648
800-395-2273

Friendship Preg. Ctrs.
484 Bloomfield Ave., # 27
Montclair, NJ 07042
973-538-0967

Friendship Preg. Ctrs.
82 Speedwell Ave.
Morristown, NJ 07960
973-538-0967

Helping Hand Preg. Ctr.
51 Trinity, PO Bx 873
Newton, NJ 07860
973-579-2272

Helping Hand PCC
326 Broad
Red Bank, NJ 07701
732-747-5454

The Open Door Preg. Ctr.
50 Hyers
Toms River, NJ 08753
732-240-5504

NEW MEXICO

Albuquerque Preg. Ctr.
2200 Menaul NE, PO Bx 27458
Albuquerque, NM 87125
505-880-0882

Deming Preg. Res. Ctr.
408 S. Platinum, PO Bx 406
Deming, NM 88031
505-544-3267

Animas CPC
1200 Schofield, PO Bx 2256
Farmington, NM 87499
505-327-4747

Gallup CPC
120 S. Boardman Dr.
Gallup, NM 87301
505-722-3445

Mesilla Valley Preg. Res. Ctr.
845 Spruce, PO Bx 1865
Las Cruces, NM 88004-1865
505-526-6242

Hope Preg. Ctr.
3500 Trinity Dr., # A-4
PO Bx 599
Los Alamos, NM 87544
505-662-2300

NEW YORK

Orleans Co. Preg. Couns. Ctr.
55 N. Main
Albion, NY 14411
716-589-7505

CPC, Schoharie Co.
44 Main, PO Bx 15
Cobleskill, NY 12043
518-234-8465

Southern Tier CPC
419 Walnut
Elmira, NY 14901
607-732-2111

PCC, Geneva
39 Seneca, PO Bx 733
Geneva, NY 14456
315-789-0708

Ithaca Preg. Ctr.
Center Ithaca, # 202, Bx 147
Ithaca, NY 14850
607-273-4673

New Paltz Preg. Support Ctr.
8 Cherry Hill Plaza
New Paltz, NY 12561
914-255-8242

Midtown Preg. Support Ctr.
104 E 40th St., # 802
New York, NY 10016
212-986-9767

Study the Options, Please
608 E. Main, PO Bx 321
Palmyra, NY 14522
315-597-2233

Pittsford Outreach Room CPC
421 Marsh Rd.
Pittsford, NY 14534
800-721-8082

Poughkeepsie CPC
46 Lincoln Ave.
Poughkeepsie, NY 12601
914-471-9284

CPC, Oneida County
607 N. Washington
Rome, NY 13440
800-662-4272

Rockland PCC (Suffern)
50A S. Main, # 203
Spring Valley, NY 10977
914-352-6074

CPC, New York
38 10th St.
Staten Island. NY 10306
718-667-4357

CPC, Oneida Co.
208 Lansing
Utica, NY 13501
800-662-4272

CPC, Oneida Co.
240 Oriskany Blvd., PO Bx 154
Whitesboro, NY 13492
800-662-4272

NORTH CAROLINA

Randolph PCC
530 S. Cox
Asheboro, NC 27203
336-629-9988

Boone CPC
232 Furman Rd., PO Bx 3316
Boone, NC 28607
704-265-4357

Preg. Support Svcs.-Chapel Hill
431 W. Franklin, # 23
Chapel Hill, NC 27516
919-942-7318

CPC, Cabarrus Co.
51 Means Ave. SE
Concord, NC 28025
704-782-2221

Preg. Support Svcs.
3500 Westgate Dr., # 401
PO Bx 52599
Durham, NC 27717-2599
919-490-0203

Greensboro & Piedmont PCCs
917 N. Elm
Greensboro, NC 27401
336-274-4881

Carolina Preg. Ctr.
209B S. Evans, PO Bx 1964
Greenville, NC 27835
919-757-0003

Reach Out CPC
1565 Gulf Rd., # B
PO Bx 186
Gulf, NC 27256
919-898-2923

Coastal PCC
70 E. Plaza
Havelock, NC 28532
919-447-2229

PCC, Catawba Valley
125 3rd St. NE, PO Bx 9423
Hickory, NC 28603
704-322-4272

PCC, High Point
212 N. Lindsay, PO Bx 6331
High Point, NC 27262
336-887-2232

Coastal PCC
148 Chaney Ave.
Jacksonville, NC 28540
910-938-7000

Ashe CPC
120A Blackburn, PO Bx 1572
Jefferson, NC 28640
336-246-4100

Coastal PCC
101 Country Aire Suites
5447 Hwy. 70 W.
Morehead City, NC 28557
919-247-2273

Craven Preg. Couns. Ctr.
1902B Brittany Pl., PO Bx 3001
New Bern, NC 28564
252-638-4673

Preg. Life Care Ctr.
1001 Navaho Dr., # 101
Raleigh, NC 27609-7318
919-873-2442

Rocky Mount Preg. Ctr.
330 Sunset Ave.
Rocky Mount, NC 27804
919-446-2273

Preg. Support Ctr.
1146 N. Main, PO Bx 81
Roxboro, NC 27573
336-503-8820

CPC, Cleveland Co.
232 S. Lafayette, PO Bx 522
Shelby, NC 28151-0522
704-487-4357

OHIO

Akron Preg. Svcs.
105 E. Market
Akron, OH 44308-2000
330-434-2221

Surburban Preg. Svcs.
3515 Manchester Rd.
Akron, OH 44319
330-644-4490

CPC, Logan Co.
110 N. Detroit, PO Bx 487
Bellefontaine, OH 43311-0487
937-592-7734

Abigail Preg. Svcs., Bellevue
108 W. Main
Bellevue, OH 44811
800-311-2022

CPC, Cleveland
398 W. Bagley Rd., # 13
Berea, OH 44017
440-243-2520

Cincinnati CPC
210 William Howard Taft Rd.
Cincinnati, OH 45219
513-961-7777

Pickaway Preg. Care
157 W. High, PO Bx 321
Circleville, OH 43113
740-477-1761

Alternaterm Preg. Svcs.
2026 Lee Rd.
Cleveland Heights, OH 44118
216-371-4848

Miami Valley Women's Ctr.
2345 W. Stroop Rd.
Dayton, OH 45439
937-298-2822

Cornerstone Preg. Svcs.
800 Middle Ave.
Elyria, OH 44035-5855
440-284-1010

Portage Co. Preg. Distress Ctr.
275 Martinel Dr., # W
Kent, OH 44240
330-673-4847

PCC, Madison Co.
51 N. Oak, PO Bx 403
London, OH 43140
740-852-0443

PCC, Union Co.
825 W. 6th St., PO Bx 682
Marysville, OH 43040
937-642-5683

Preg. Help Ctr., N. Cincinnati
106 N. East St.
Mason, OH 45040-1746
513-398-7175

Middletown Area CPC
2230 Central Ave.
Middletown, OH 45044
513-424-2229

Knox Preg. Svcs.
116 E. High, PO Bx 606
Mount Vernon, OH 43050
740-393-0370

Abigail Preg. Svcs.
22 W. Main
Norwalk, OH 44857
800-311-2022

CPC, Oxford
23 E. High
Oxford, OH 45056
513-523-1814

CPC, Springfield
1027 Mitchell Blvd.
Springfield, OH 45503
937-390-1335

Sycamore House Preg. Ctr., Champaign Co.
315 Sycamore, PO Bx 775
Urbana, OH 43078
937-653-3737

Abigail Preg. Svcs., Willard
302 Woodland Ave., # 301
Willard, OH 44890
800-311-2022

Clinton Co. Women's Ctr.
132 E. Main
Wilmington, OH 45177
937-382-2424

PCC, Wayne Co.
2330 Cleveland Rd.
Wooster, OH 44691
330-264-5880

CPC, Mahoning Co.
5385 Market
Youngstown, OH 44512
330-788-4000

OKLAHOMA

CPS, Atoka
111 E. A St., PO Bx 426
Atoka, OK 74525
888-981-5683

The Caring Ctr.
1809 Jefferson
Bartlesville, OK 74006
918-335-1076

Cleveland Co. Preg Ctr.
113 Elm Ave., PO Bx 2803
Norman, OK 73070-2803
405-579-4673

OREGON

Albany CPC
409 First Ave. W.
Albany, OR 97321
541-924-0166

Lower Columbia CPC
1213 Franklin
Astoria, OR 97103
503-325-9111

Rachel Ctr. Crisis Preg. Help
2504 10th St., PO Bx 1086
Baker City, OR 97814
541-523-5357

Beaverton CPC
4700 SW Watson
Beaverton, OR 97005
503-643-4503

CPCs, Central OR, Bend
1007½ NW Galveston
PO Bx 8208
Bend, OR 97708
800-499-4673

CPCs, N. Willamette Valley
149 N Holly
Canby, OR 97013
503-266-2673

Caring Preg. Ctr.
840 Central Ave.
Coos Bay, OR 97420
541-267-5204

Lane Preg. Support Ctr.
134 E. 13th Ave, # 5
Eugene, OR 97401
541-998-7920

Gresham CPC
104 NW 11th Ave.
Gresham, OR 97030
503-666-6527

Preg. Crisis Support
Women's Care Ctr.
2415 N. First St., PO Bx 1531
Hermiston, OR 97838
541-567-0888

Mid-Columbia CPC
914 Eugene, PO Bx 697
Hood River, OR 97031
541-386-1050

CPCs, Central OR, Madras
116 SE D St., # B, PO Bx 55
Madras, OR 97741
800-499-4673

Preg. Couns. & Info. Ctr.
101 S. Baker, PO Bx 945
McMinnville, OR 97128
503-434-4400

Milwaukie CPC
14419 SE McLoughlin Blvd.
Milwaukie, OR 97267
503-659-3336

CPCs, N. Willamette Valley
31268 S. Short Fellows Rd.
Molalla, OR 97038
503-824-2673

CPCs, N. Willamette Valley
217 N. Molalla Ave., PO Bx 129
Molalla, OR 97038
503-829-2673

Intermountain CPC
588 W. Idaho Ave., PO Bx 400
Ontario, OR 97914
541-889-4272

Pendleton Preg. Crisis Support
17 SW Frazer Ave., # 228
Pendleton, OR 97801
541-276-5757

CPCs, Portland Metro Area
3105 NE Weidler
Portland, OR 97232-1830
503-284-1830

Lloyd Ctr. CPC
1616 NE 9th Ave.
Portland, OR 97232-1210
503-284-1977

CPCs, Central OR, Prineville
312 N. Deer
Prineville, OR 97754
800-499-4673

CPCs, Central OR, Redmond
1240 SW Glacier, # 2 & 5
PO Bx 1312
Redmond, OR 97756
800-499-4673

Hope Preg. Ctr.
1533 NE Vine
Roseburg, OR 97470-1541
541-672-2609

Salem Pregnancy Ctr.
2630 Market NE, PO Bx 5302
Salem OR 97304
503-364-2464

Columbia Preg. Ctr.
135 N. 6th St., PO Bx 344
St. Helens, OR 97051
503-397-6047

Mid-Columbia CPC-T.D.
1501 W. First St.
The Dalles, OR 97058
541-296-1541

Lake Grove CPC
17937 SW McEwan Rd.
Tigard, OR 97224-7729
503-968-6780

PENNSYLVANIA

Lehigh Valley CPC
27 S. 8th St.
Allentown, PA 18101
610-821-4000

The Ark PCC
615 Broad Ave.
Belle Vernon, PA 15012
724-929-2930

Bradford PCC
2 Main, # 115
Bradford, PA 16701
800-395-4357

Amnion CPC
944 Haverford Rd.
Bryn Mawr, PA 19010
610-525-1557

Capital Area Preg. Ctr.
2509 Old Gettysburg Rd.
Camp Hill, PA 17011
717-761-4411

Endless Mountains PCC
8 W. Main, PO Bx 42
Canton, PA 17724
800-326-9953

Preg. Ministries
497 Lincoln Way E., PO Bx 941
Chambersburg, PA 17201-0941
717-267-3738

AAA Preg. Ctr.
214 S. 7th Ave., PO Bx 401
Clarion, PA 16214
814-226-7007

Easton CPC
133 N. 4th St.
Easton, PA 18042
610-559-9327

Cornerstone PCS
5287 Lincoln Hwy., PO Bx 576
Gap, PA 17527
800-337-9306

Tender Care Preg. Ctr.
354 York
Gettysburg, PA 17325-1930
800-348-0088

Greenville Regional Preg. Ctr.
331 Main
Greenville, PA 16125
724-588-2229

Tender Care Preg. Ctr.
966 Carlisle
Hanover, PA 17331
800-348-0088

CPC, Kutztown
443 W. Main
Kutztown, PA 19530
610-683-8000

PCC, Susquehanna Valley
9 N. 3rd St.
Lewisburg, PA 17837
800-395-4357

Preg. Ctr., Meadville
657 Pine
Meadville, PA 16335
814-333-6567

Beaver Valley P. Support Ctr.
110 Christy Dr.
Monaca, PA 15061
724-728-5550

Airport Area PCC
358 Flaugherty Run Rd.
PO Bx 1142
Moon Township, PA 15108-1142
724-457-1220

Preg. Care Ctr.
449 E. Washington
New Castle, PA 16101
724-658-6329

Small Beginnings Preg. Ctr.
137 Locust, PO Bx 207
Oxford, PA 19363
800-337-9306

Allegheny PCC
2436 Calif. Ave.
Pittsburgh, PA 15212
412-323-2273

Central Pittsburgh PCC
211 N. Whitfield, #480
Pittsburgh, PA 15206
412-661-8430

N. Pittsburgh PCC (adm.)
238 West View Ave., Bx 15034
Pittsburgh, PA 15237
412-931-8405

Oakland PCC
c/o Bellefield Presb. Church
4001 5th Ave.
Pittsburgh, PA 15213
412-661-8430

South Hills CPC
4166 Library Rd.
Pittsburgh, PA 15234
412-531-2112

Genesis CPC
151 King
Pottstown, PA 19464
610-970-8088

Crossroads Preg. Care
1313 W. Broad
Quakertown, PA 18951
215-538-7003

Preg. Ministries
124 W. King, # 1
Shippensburg, PA 17257
800-638-0743

CPC, Poconos
115 N. 8th St.
Stroudsburg, PA 18360-1719
717-424-1113

CPC, Wyoming Co.
134 E. Tioga
Tunkhannock, PA 18657
717-836-4440

Preg. Ministries
237 E. Main
Waynesboro, PA 17268
800-638-0743

N. Pittsburgh PCC
10263 Perry Hwy.
Wexford, PA 15090
412-931-8405

PCC, Susquehanna Valley
57 E. 4th St.
Williamsport, PA 17701
800-395-4357

Human Life Svcs.
742 S. George
York, PA 17403-3133
717-846-2384

RHODE ISLAND

South Co. CPC
94 Main
Wakefield, RI 02879
401-783-7725

SOUTH CAROLINA

Aiken PCC
130 Waterloo, PO Bx 3294
Aiken, SC 29802
803-649-9890

Lowcountry CPC
2810 Ashley Phosphate Rd., # B-10
Charleston, SC 29418-6406
803-553-3505

Hope Women's Center
879 Gentry Memorial Hwy.
PO Bx 225
Easley, SC 29641-0225
864-855-8500

Piedmont Women's Ctr.
1146 Grove Rd.
Greenville, SC 29605
864-233-3823

Piedmont Women's Ctr., L.
710 Laurens Rd.
Greenville, SC 29607
864-233-3823

Piedmont Women's Ctr.
Adm., PO Bx 8543
Greenville, SC 29604-8543
864-233-3823

Piedmont Women's Ctr., Greer
506 N Main
Greer, SC 29650
864-233-3823

AA York Co. CPC
828 Lucas, PO Bx 4302
Rock Hill, SC 29732
803-329-2524

Foothills CPC
321 E. Main, PO Bx 2103
Seneca, SC 29679-2103
864-882-8797

SOUTH DAKOTA

Black Hills CPC
520 Kansas City, # 307
Rapid City, SD 57701
605-341-4477

Alpha Ctr.
801 E. 41st St.
Sioux Falls, SD 57105
605-335-8631

Northern Hills PCC
1231 Polley Dr., # 9, PO Bx 755
Spearfish, SD 57783-0755
605-642-4140

TENNESSEE

AAA Women's Svcs.
744 McCallie Ave., # 427
Chattanooga, TN 37403
423-892-0803

AAA Women's Svcs.
6232 Vance Rd.
Chattanooga, TN 37421
423-892-0803

Crisis Preg. Support Ctr.
325 N. 2nd St., PO Bx 44
Clarksville, TN 37040
931-645-2273

Women's Care Ctr.
1332 Market
Dayton, TN 37321
423-775-0019

CPC, Middle TN
101 W. Railroad, PO Bx 765
Dickson, TN 37056
615-446-0701

Hope Resource Center
2700 Painter Ave.
Knoxville, TN 37919
423-525-4673

Agape House PCC
210 Oakland, PO Bx 473
Martin, TN 38237
901-588-0305

Middle TN Crisis Preg.
Support Ctr.
106 E. College, PO Bx 5023
Murfreesboro, TN 37133
615-221-0627

TEXAS

Amarillo Area CPCs
1600 S. Coulter, # 203
PO Bx 50342
Amarillo, TX 79121
806-354-2244

First Heartbeat CPC
301 Amarillo Blvd. W., # 205
Amarillo, TX 79107
806-376-6298

LifeCare Preg. Svcs.
611 Carpenter Ave., # 201
Austin, TX 78753
512-835-2343

CPC, Baytown
519 Park, PO Bx 8202
Baytown, TX 77522
281-427-2273

Hill Country PCC
919 N. Main, PO Bx 205
Boerne, TX 78006
830-249-9717

Borger Area CPC
408 W. Adams, PO Bx 5641
Borger, TX 79008-5641
806-273-8373

Hope Preg. Ctrs., Brazos Valley
3620 E. 29th St.
Bryan, TX 77802
409-846-1097

Burleson Preg. Aid Ctr.
509D SW Wilshire Blvd.
Burleson, TX 76028
817-295-4101

Canyon CPC
1709 5th Ave., rear
Canyon, TX 79015
806-655-4673

Corpus Christi Preg. Ctr.
4730 Everhart Rd.
Corpus Christi, TX 78411
512-991-2008

Ctr. for Pregnancy
217C E. Parkwood, PO Bx 1202
Friendswood, TX 77546
281-482-5683

CPC, Central
3636 San Jacinto, PO Bx 740444
Houston, TX 77274-0444
713-526-7878

CPC, Houston
5615 Richmond Ave, # 125
Houston, TX 77057-6320
713-780-0030

CPC, Westheimer
13155 Westheimer, # 136
Houston, TX 77077
281-531-5655

Family Assist. Ctr.
3806 Live Oak, PO Bx 35522
Houston, TX 77235
713-726-9476

Women's Preg. Ctr.
8300 Bissonnet, # 160
Houston, TX 77074
713-774-0126

Preg. Help Ctr., W. Houston
20501 Katy Fwy., # 240
Katy, TX 77450
281-599-0909

Preg. Ctr., Kerrville
829 Earl Garrett, PO Bx 1832
Kerrville, TX 78028
830-257-2166

Parkridge Preg. Ctr.
5203 79th St., # B
Lubbock, TX 79424
800-687-4444

New Braunfels CPC
1281 E. Common
PO Bx 311342
New Braunfels, TX 78131-1342
830-629-7565

Top O' Texas CPC
108 E. Browning, PO Bx 2097
Pampa, TX 79066-2097
806-669-2229

CPS, Central Plains
1209 Quincy, PO Bx 189
Plainview, TX 79073
800-215-4284

Women-to-Women
700 E. Park Blvd, # 206
Plano, TX 75074
972-424-0767

Christian Pro-Life Foundation
7909 Fredericksburg Rd, # 233
San Antonio, TX 78229
210-614-4124

Women's Preg. Ctr.
202 CM Allen Pkwy., # 7
PO Bx 304
San Marcos, TX 78667
512-396-3020

Grayson Co. CPC
412 W. Lamar, PO Bx 3237
Sherman, TX 75091-3237
800-552-9099

Northwest Preg. Ctr.
16000 Stuebner-Airline, # 260
Spring, TX 77379
281-320-8788

Preg. Assist. Ctr. N.
26402 I-45 N
Spring, TX 77386
281-367-1518

Cross Timbers PCC
1902 W. Sloan, PO Bx 163
Stephenville, TX 76401
254-965-6031

Hope Preg. Ctr.
1610 S. 31st St., # 200
Temple, TX 76504
254-778-8119

AngelCare Preg. Res. Ctr.
2130 N. 33rd St.
Waco, TX 76708
254-753-5753

UTAH

The Care Ctr.
271 N. 100 W., PO Bx 333
Brigham City, UT 84302-0333
435-723-0500

PCC, Ogden
3701 S. Harrison Blvd.
Ogden, UT 84403
801-621-4357

Preg. Res. Ctr., Salt Lake
805 E. 900 S., PO Bx 526276
Salt Lake City, UT 84152-6276
801-363-5433

VERMONT

Central VT Preg. Svcs.
122 N. Main, PO Bx 513
Barre, VT 05641-0513
802-479-9215

Tri-State Preg. Ctr.
450 Main, PO Bx 1084
Bennington, VT 05201
800-395-4357

Lifeway Preg. Ctr.
218 Canal
Brattleboro, VT 05301
802-254-6734

Burlington CPS
56 Colchester Ave.
Burlington, VT 05401
800-395-4357

PCC, Addison Co.
Route 7, 8 Court St.
RR 4, Bx 2051, # 1
Middlebury, VT 05753
802-388-7272

First Step Preg. Ctr.
Gryphon Building, # 207
56½ Merchants Row
Rutland, VT 05701
800-395-4357

VIRGINIA

Charlottesville Preg. Ctr.
2244 Ivy Rd, # 1
Charlottesville, VA 22903
804-979-8888

Culpepper Preg. Ctr.
420 Sunset Lane
Culpepper, VA 22701
540-727-0400

Shenandoah Co. Preg. Ctr.
82 Landfill Rd.
Edinburg, VA 22824
540-984-4673

Southside Preg. Ctr.
142 N. Main, PO Bx 281
Farmville, VA 23901
804-392-8483

Rappahannock Preg. Help Ctr.
1901 Plank Rd.
Fredericksburg, VA 22401
888-886-5786

Peninsula CPC
2019 Cunningham Dr, # 402
PO Bx 7868
Hampton, VA 23666
757-827-0303

Page Preg. Assistance Ctr.
315 W. Main
Luray, VA 22835
540-743-1464

CPCs, Pr. Wm. & Fauquier Cos.
8741 Plantation Ln., PO Bx 2040
Manassas, VA 20108
703-330-1300

Tri-Cities CPC
1360 E. Washington
Petersburg, VA 23803-3467
804-861-5433

CPC, Metro. Richmond
3202 W. Cary, # 200
Richmond, VA 23221-3402
804-353-2320

Preg. Help Ctr.
1409 N. Augusta, PO Bx 924
Staunton, VA 24402-0924
540-885-6261

Preg. Help Ctr., Waynesboro
1305 13th St.
Waynesboro, VA 22980
540-943-1700

Warrenton CPC
578 Waterloo Rd, # 4A
Warrenton, VA 20186
540-347-7770

ABBA PCC
2438 Valley Ave.
Winchester, VA 22601
540-665-9660

WASHINGTON

Whatcom Co. Preg. Ctr.
1308 N. State, PO Bx 1663
Bellingham, WA 98227
360-671-9057

CPC, Camas-Washougal
1542 NE 3rd Ave., PO Bx 1036
Camas, WA 98607
360-834-2829

Care Center, Lewis Co.
604 W. Main, PO Bx 987
Centralia, WA 98531-0987
360-330-2229

Colville Preg. Ctr.
973 E. Birch Ave., PO Bx 551
Colville, WA 99114
509-684-9895

Ellensburg PCC
409 N. Pine, PO Bx 740
Ellensburg, WA 98926
509-925-2273

CPCs of Snohomish Co.
Adm. Ofc., PO Bx 5634
Everett, WA 98206
425-355-0693

Everett CPC & The Care Van
6833 Evergreen Way
Everett, WA 98203
425-347-0837

Caring Place, W. Clallam Co.
260 Ash Ave., PO Bx 2111
Forks, WA 98331
360-374-5010

CPC, Goldendale
101½ Main, PO Bx 227
Goldendale, WA 98620
509-773-5501

Lower Valley Preg. Ctr.
204 W. 2nd St., PO Bx 312
Grandview, WA 98930
509-882-1899

Lower Columbia CPC
118 First, # 4, PO Bx 837
Ilwaco, WA 98624
360-642-8717

Lynnwood CPC
5017 196th St. SW, # 206
Lynnwood, WA 98036
425-774-7850

CPC, Skagit Co.
617 W. Division
Mt. Vernon, WA 98273-3219
360-428-4777

Hannah House PCC
1152 2nd Ave. N., PO Bx 428
Okanogan, WA 98840
509-422-5506

CPC, Thurston Co.
1416 State Ave. NE
Olympia, WA 98506
360-753-0061

Tri-Cities Preg. Ctr.
817 N. 14th St., # B, PO Bx 4701
Pasco, WA 99302-4701
509-544-9329

CPC, Clallam Co.
535 E. 8th St., PO Bx 39
Port Angeles, WA 98362
360-452-3309

CPC, Clallam Co., Sequim
665 N. 5th Ave, PO Bx 39
Port Angeles, WA 98362
360-452-3309

CPC, Pierce Co.
10312 120th St. E, # 8
Puyallup, WA 98374
253-770-8697

Tri-Cities Preg. Ctr.
636 Jadwin, # C
Richland, WA 99352
509-943-2124

PCC, Mason Co.
706 Cascade Ave., PO Bx 1581
Shelton, WA 98584
360-427-9171

CPCs, Spokane
539 W. Sharp, # C
Spokane, WA 99201-2422
509-327-0701

CPCs, Spokane-Valley
12012 E. Sprague, # 3A
Spokane, WA 99212
509-327-0701

CPC, Pierce Co.
1209 6th Ave.
Tacoma, WA 98405
253-383-2988

CPC, Yakima
305 S. 11th Ave, # 3, PO Bx 644
Yakima, WA 98907-0644
509-248-2273

WASHINGTON, D.C.
See DISTRICT OF COLUMBIA; MARYLAND; VIRGINIA

WISCONSIN

Apple PCC
2600 Stein Blvd.
Eau Claire, WI 54701
715-834-7734

New Hope Preg. Ctr.
2222 Roosevelt Rd.
Kenosha, WI 53143
414-658-2222

Preg. Resource Ctr.
105 E. Miner Ave.
Ladysmith, WI 54848
800-657-4919

Preg. Info. Ctr.
1605 Monroe
Madison WI 53711
608-259-1605

Affiliated CPC
2917 N. Oakland Ave.
Milwaukee, WI 53211
414-962-2212

Preg. Ctr., Green Co.
1508 11th St., PO Bx 13
Monroe, WI 53566-0013
608-325-5051

Door of Hope PCC
210 N. Main, PO Bx 3
Viroqua, WI 54665
608-637-8777

WYOMING

LifeChoice
520 E. 18th St.
Cheyenne, WY 82001
307-632-6659

CPC, Jackson Hole
250 E. Pearl, PO Bx 436
Jackson Hole, WY 83001
307-733-5162

Albany Co. Caring Ctr.
869 N. 4th St.
Laramie, WY 82070
307-745-3444

ABBA's House
108 S. 7th E., PO Bx 1242
Riverton, WY 82501
800-459-0999

The Authors

Linda Roggow, a supervisor of social services at New Horizons Adoption Agency in Minnesota and Iowa, is a licensed social worker (LSW). She earned her master's degree in social work (MSW) from the University of Hawaii and has been working in the adoption field for over fifteen years.

In counseling unwed mothers, Roggow looked for a book that did not offer abortion as a good alternative. She could not find one, so she wrote this book, now in its third edition. It has helped many young women and their families. She has been instrumental in starting several Care Net Pregnancy Care Centers in Midwestern United States.

Linda Roggow and her husband, a dentist, live in Jackson, Minnesota. They have traveled extensively, backpacking through the Far East, Europe, and Scandinavia. They have a daughter and son.

Roggow attends Our Savior Evangelical Lutheran Church, teaches Sunday school, and is active in church and community activities.

Carolyn Owens, a library clerk, has written fifteen children's activity books and many articles. She belongs to the Minnesota Christian Writers Guild. Carolyn and her husband live in Minneapolis and have two grown daughters. They attend the Church of the Open Door.